THE LITTLE POCKET BOOK OF
HAPPINESS

HOW TO LOVE LIFE, LAUGH MORE, AND LIVE LONGER

Swap worry and anxiety for joy and contentment
and unlock the secrets to a happier way of being

LOIS BLYTH

CICO BOOKS
LONDON NEW YORK

Published in 2015 by CICO Books
An imprint of Ryland Peters & Small Ltd

20–21 Jockey's Fields   341 E 116th St
London WC1R 4BW   New York, NY 10029

www.rylandpeters.com

10 9 8 7 6

First published in 2013 as *The Secrets of Happiness*

Text © Sarah Sutton 2013
Design and illustration © CICO Books 2015

A CIP catalog record for this book is available from the Library of
Congress and the British Library.

ISBN: 978 1 78249 260 3

Printed in China

Editor: Marion Paull
Designer: Jerry Goldie
Illustrator: Amy Louise Evans

In-house editor: Anna Galkina
In-house designer: Fahema Khanam
Art director: Sally Powell
Production controller: Sarah Kulasek-Boyd
Publishing manager: Penny Craig
Publisher: Cindy Richards

CONTENTS

INTRODUCTION

Happiness is like a riddle. The more we want it and the more we seek it, the more elusive it becomes. And yet, when we are least conscious of looking for it, it can envelop us in a warm sense of contentment and belonging, making a single moment precious and valuable beyond measure. A feeling of happiness has the power to light up our whole being. It is elemental. It can be triggered by the smallest event. Scientists will tell us that it has the power to heal and to extend life. It is the ingredient we all seek to make our lives complete. Like the air we breathe, we are not conscious that we need it, until it disappears. Happiness makes us feel glad to be alive.

Why are some people happy and others not? People may be healthy and wealthy beyond measure but still feel discontented or unhappy. Are we born happy? Can we learn to be happy? Where does it come from and how can we live happier and more contented lives? There is no single path to happiness, because everyone views the world slightly differently, and each person's road to contentment is unique.

The happiness habit is an easy one to acquire. The difficult bit for some is choosing to step away from un-happiness and deciding, wholeheartedly, and with total commitment, that happiness is something that you really do want—and that you deserve. The challenge for others is choosing to step out of the place of comfort and familiarity and to start experiencing new challenges that inspire you to live your life in a different and vibrant way.

Happiness requires you to adopt a new way of seeing the events in your life, involving a willingness to let go of the past and to recognize that things don't happen to you—they just happen. Personal disappointments and tragedies can have such a profoundly numbing effect that it is possible to put your life on hold—for years. But even in our darkest hours we can choose to see the glimmer of light that tells us there is joy to be had, in every situation, and there is the promise of a happier outcome, if we choose to look for it.

The Little Pocket Book of Happiness offers you a more joyous approach to living and thinking; a shift that may reframe your view of the world. It shows you simple things you can decide to do, consciously, so that now becomes the time when you can start to be happier. It includes strategies to warm the heart and open the mind to the extraordinary power of happiness. The good news is that happiness is within everyone's grasp. It has the power to transform, heal, and restore life to one that is worth living.

The Little Pocket Book of Happiness has a simple mission— to offer hope to those who feel that happiness is eluding them; to offer ways of thinking about the state of happiness that can create a sense of joy and contentment; and to encourage those who are happy to value, share, and discover more ways to live a truly fulfilled and enjoyable life. In the words of Max Ehrmann's Desiderata, "Be careful. Strive to be happy."

Identity and Freedom

"We hold these truths to be self-evident, that all men are created equal, that they are endowed by their Creator with certain unalienable Rights, that among these are Life, Liberty and the pursuit of Happiness."

The Declaration of Independence, July 4, 1776.

The pursuit of happiness is part of our identity as human beings. For Americans, it is part of national identity, embedded in the heart of the United States' Declaration of Independence. The Declaration, signed after a long period of war and disagreement, confirmed the desire of the 13 States to become independent of the British Empire. Part of the US government's responsibility to the people remains, "to effect their Safety and Happiness."

At government level, the concept of happiness is synonymous with a desire for freedom.

CHAPTER I

WHAT IS HAPPINESS?

DISCOVER THE HAPPINESS HABIT

"There is no way to happiness; happiness is the way."
Buddhist proverb

Have you smiled at yourself in the mirror lately? Did the smile come easily, or did it feel as if the muscles in your face need a little exercise?

Most young children are happiness magnets. All they need is love, safety, and space to play to create a world where fun is but a laugh and a smile away. As we grow older many people lose the happiness habit; they swap fun and spontaneity for professional aspirations and personal responsibilities. Pressure of time leads to living life in a rush, with face tense and very little time to "stop and stare"; tasks

If you want happiness for an hour; take a nap.

If you want happiness for a day; go fishing.

If you want happiness for a month; get married.

If you want happiness for a year; inherit a fortune.

If you want happiness for a lifetime; help someone else.

Chinese saying

become chores rather than achievements; true happiness becomes a rare commodity saved for weekends, vacations, and special occasions.

You don't need to reach a full-blown state of un-happiness to be aware that you would prefer your life to be more joyful, more relaxed, or more fulfilling. The signals show up in body language and the things we do and say. How often have you heard a less-than-happy person say, "I wish …," "I should have …," "If only …," "I can't because …," "You're lucky …," "I'm so tired …" followed by a frown and a deep sigh?

The danger is that discontent can become a familiar reflex. It is all too easy to drift along in a state of grumbling dissatisfaction, sometimes for years, blaming circumstances, waiting for something to happen, and finding every excuse not to make the changes that could transform life and make you happier.

Read on to discover whether you have invested in one of the Myths of Happiness and how you can choose a new way of approaching your future.

smile, smile, smile, smile, smile, smile, smile,

IF I WAS RICH, I WOULD BE HAPPIER

"Trying to be happy by accumulating possessions is like trying to satisfy hunger by taping sandwiches all over your body."
George Carlin

Happiness expert Srikumar Rao believes that we spend most of our lives learning to be unhappy instead of enjoying the pleasure of feeling vibrantly alive. This is because we spend so much time thinking about what we have to get before we can be happy; and because we tell ourselves we have failed if the outcome is not exactly as we expect it to be. We tell ourselves IF we have a better job, more money, a nicer house, a more attractive partner, a better car, THEN we will be happy.

The flaw in this argument, as he points out, is that anything you get, you can also lose—at which point not only are you are left without it, you also become unhappy, and you probably blame yourself for the loss.

As long as we are attaching importance to things external to ourselves—and as long as we are intent on criticizing the present and contrasting it with an idealized future—we will always be discontented. The closer we get to our

destination, the more we will want to
upgrade to something else, so will never
reach the place where happiness is. We
will never truly see and appreciate
what we already have.

Contrast this with the way we
feel when we see a beautiful
rainbow, or a sunset, or something
of beauty in the natural world. The
effect on most people will be to "stop and stare" and to experience a moment of
stillness and wonder. In Rao's words, in that moment of appreciation you are truly
happy because, "You accepted the Universe exactly as it was," with no hint of
criticism or wishing it was somewhere else or somehow different.

THE EXPERIENCE OF LIVING SIMPLY

If you had only 24 hours left on this earth, would you go shopping or would you
want to spend time with those you care about?

Money can't buy happiness, although it can, of course, buy fun, thrills, and
enjoyment in the short-term. The culture of acquiring possessions, home-making,
and dressing well is rooted deep within our psyche and very few people would be
willing to give it all up and to choose a non-material way of life in order to achieve
happiness. However, material possessions are passive. They cannot love us, or talk
to us, or make us laugh—but they do have the potential to leave us comparing

what we have with others, and so to feed dissatisfaction, encouraging us to feel nothing will ever be enough.

Take time, right now, to consider all the non-material things that you have to be grateful for. During the course of your life, what or who has made you smile, laugh, feel loved, feel alive, feel curious, feel happy?

* Are you thinking about your love of music, running, climbing, singing, reading, dancing?

* Are you appreciating your friends, your family, your lover, your children?

* Are you remembering places you have visited, the beauty you have seen, the air you have breathed?

* Are you imagining the joy of a kiss, a scent, a taste, or a feeling?

* Are you treasuring a memory of someone no longer here?

The natural pleasures that we enjoy for free make us happy without dissatisfaction or judgment.   It is enough that they are there. These are the riches that make us truly happy; and this is the kind of happiness that makes us truly rich.

IF I HAD A BETTER JOB, I WOULD BE HAPPIER

"Success is getting what you want.
Happiness is wanting what you get."

Dale Carnegie

There is great joy to be had in working hard to achieve something, or putting in effort to earn a reward. Few people would look around at the home they have created, or consider the task they have completed, or the exams they have passed, and think to themselves, "I really wish I hadn't had such success!" Most of us are justifiably proud of our achievements and the effort that went into reaching the outcome. Achievement is inspiring. Moments of celebration lift everyone's spirits. Good news helps others to think about what is possible, too.

Nowhere is this more obvious than in sport or adventure. When the first man on the moon, astronaut Neil Armstrong, died, thousands of adults recollected the impact the moon landings had had on their own lives. When millions of people around the world watch the Olympic Games, they are united in their desire for their favored competitor to win. Success, like so many of life's experiences, is enriched when it is shared.

Why, then, are so many successful people unhappy and dissatisfied with their lives? Why, when we strive so hard to be successful, does it not always bring us joy? Why do so many successful people consider themselves to be failures?

Darwin told us that the future of all species depends on the survival of the fittest; from birth we are rewarded for things we do well and are encouraged to be the best we can be. In the work place, results are rewarded with a promotion or a pay rise. Human beings are naturally competitive and striving to become the best we can be can bring great prizes. We become extremely attached to our achievements. They define us.

When we invest more in our status than in our joy of work, several things happen:

* Fear of failure may lead us to play safe, leading to boredom and lack of personal growth.

* Over time, our work goals and our life goals may start to conflict rather than support one another.

* We may become detached from the task, or may dislike or resent it.

* We may continue in a profession because we are good at what we do, and it is comfortable, rather than because we feel joy in our work.

* If we lose status or are made redundant, we lose our sense of self, because so much has been invested in the role. It can take years to build up confidence and self-esteem once again.

* Many people in high-pressured jobs feel that they need to carry the weight upon their shoulders and do everything themselves. They feel they can't ask for help. They overlook the fact that the greatest successes are achieved as a team.

Rather than investing in an outcome over which you cannot possibly have full control, the secret of happiness is to focus instead on the process of achievement, recognizing that each step is an achievement in its own right, and each marks progress on the way to reaching your ultimate goal. The key to getting a better job is first to focus on the one you have and to do it to the best of your ability.

THE JOY OF THE TASK

Like all the secrets of happiness, the pathway to finding happiness at work begins in the mind. Try this exercise both to change your mindset and discover what kind of work would make you happier.

1 Before you go to sleep tonight, find something positive to say or think about going to work in the morning and write it down. It doesn't matter how large or small that thing is. It need have nothing to do with the work itself; you might enjoy the journey to work, bantering with colleagues or being paid at the end of the month. Whatever it is, write it down.

2 When you wake up the following day, pay attention to how you feel about going to work. Is your first thought positive or negative? If it is positive, write it down. If it is negative, read the positive thought you had last night and think again. Can you swap your positive for a negative? Write that down. Even extreme negatives can be reframed into positives. Instead of "I hate my job," try thinking, "Knowing how unhappy I am in my work shows me that I would be better suited to work that is …" (Only you can fill in the gap.)

3 Think about each task that you have to complete during each day and focus on how good it feels to complete each one. Acknowledge to yourself how well you have done and consider how you could do it even better next time.

4 If you keep this up over the period of a month, three things will happen. First, you will have a list of at least 60 things that make you feel happy and positive about your job that you will have repeated every day; second, you will notice more things about your work that you enjoy, which will make you feel happier at work, and will make others react more positively toward you. Thirdly, if you are still unhappy, you will know much more about what kind of work would suit you better.

Creativity expert Sir Ken Robinson has written extensively about the importance of having a passion for what you do. When your work is your passion, the lines between work and leisure blur, and you are aware of enjoying your life and loving what you do. Considering that we spend a great percentage of our lives working, we owe it to ourselves to be as happy at work as we can be. Of course, it is not always possible to make a living from the skill you most value or enjoy—and sometimes it is more fun to keep your passion as a hobby, so you can pursue it on your own terms. For some people the joy of the task comes from the work itself; for others it is all about their colleagues, the banter, and the environment. The underlying principle is that there are always ways, means, and colleagues who can turn a basic chore into fun; or a major challenge into an adventure.

can you swap your negative for a positive?

IF I WAS MORE ATTRACTIVE, I WOULD BE HAPPIER

"People are like stained-glass windows. They sparkle and shine when the sun is out, but when the darkness sets in, their true beauty is revealed only if there is a light from within."

Elisabeth Kübler-Ross

We live in a world where office workers choose to undergo minor cosmetic enhancements during their lunch hour; where celebrities of every age pay extraordinary amounts to get their breasts, buttocks, noses, and other body parts restructured, when no one else had noticed their presumed flaws. Thousands of people around the world who are blessed with beauty are unhappy with the way they look and think that losing weight, gaining weight, buying a designer sweater, or changing their hair color will somehow make them feel better about themselves. Children as young as ten are suffering from eating disorders. What on earth is going on? Have we reached a point where we value looks over substance? Youth over ageing? At what point did beauty start to mean everyone has to try to look the same?

At what point did beauty start to mean everyone has to try to look the same?

On one level, this complex subject is quite simple—we cannot see ourselves as others see us. We see ourselves only when we look in a mirror or look at a photograph. How can we notice the light in our eyes when we are looking out of them, not into them? How can we see the energy in our step when we are inside our body?

Each of us is a unique human being, and we are changing both physically and emotionally all the time. The chances are that no one will remember in five years' time what color dress you wore to a particular event; or whether your hair was too long or too short. They may not even remember what you said. What they will remember is whether they enjoyed your company; and whether your company made them feel good about themselves, too.

The truth in the myth is not that "If I was more attractive, I would be happier," but "If I was happier, I would be more attractive." That starts with valuing yourself for who you are.

THE EYES HAVE IT

I challenge you to delve into an old photo album that you haven't looked at in years and take a fresh look at the photos of yourself when you were 20 years younger. How attractive did you feel then? The chances are you felt the same way as you do now, but in looking back you will see how lovely you were. Were you any happier with your appearance? Probably not.

Now imagine how you will react in 20 years' time when you look back at photos of yourself today, and do the same exercise again. Really feel it.

Next look in the mirror at your present-day self and smile as if you are looking at someone you care about. Look at the lines around your eyes that tell the world how you smile; look at the lines that tell the story of your life; and look at the way your face lights up when you smile. Your older self can look back in appreciation at how beautiful you are right now.

The person who lights up a room is not the one who is the most physically beautiful, but the one whose inner light brightens the lives of those around them.

IF MY LOVE LOVED ME,
I WOULD BE HAPPIER

*"Think not you can direct the course of love, for love,
if it finds you worthy, directs your course."*

Kahlil Gibran

There is truth in this myth. When two people share an intensity of feeling, the heart sings and we feel capable of anything. The feeling of being loved does make us happier, but not all kinds of love are sustainable, and when love changes its form, we cannot demand that someone loves us back in the same way.

Much of life is about loving and losing and learning how to give and take in relationships. When a relationship ends it can feel as if life is over and that you will never laugh, smile, or be ready for love again. Unrequited love can be

> What we can do is share moments in time that send the heart soaring and bring us to life; moments that we can treasure for a lifetime.

equally painful, leaving the person who feels unloved consumed with a sense of loss that can become debilitating and sometimes self-destructive. Love is a gift that can bring as much pain as it does joy. It can take courage to pick yourself up, dust yourself off, and start all over again.

But, of course, your love was never *your* love. We do not belong to one another. We cannot be owned. What we can do is share moments in time that send the heart soaring and bring us to life; moments that we can treasure for a lifetime.

Choosing Love Over Sadness

* Love is not a finite pot of feeling. There is always room for more. Instead of telling yourself that you will never love anyone ever again, try thinking, "I will never stop loving the person I have loved. Even though I am in pain at the moment, my heart is open to loving someone new in time."

* Spend time with friends and family who love and appreciate you. Their kindness may make you more acutely aware of the one you are missing, but their support will help you to accept what has passed and move on.

＊ Time passes. There is a cliché that time heals all things, and in the case of heartbreak it is true. One day you will wake up to find that something has shifted. You feel free to be yourself again. Instead of wanting to hang on to what you had, you will see why you had to let it go. Trust in the process and you will find your way back to happiness.

Eros: Love Eternal

The Ancient Greeks believed that erotic love was a form of madness. The Greek god, Eros, is characterized by his bow and arrow, as he shoots painful darts into the hearts of those afflicted by passion. But interestingly, the concept of eros as a form of love has nothing to do with physical beauty. Whereas physical beauty fades, eros is considered to be eternal—which just goes to show, happiness, like beauty, is more than skin deep.

MY LIFE IS UNFAIR—
I WILL NEVER BE HAPPY

"Everything can be taken from a man but one thing: the last of the human freedoms—to choose one's attitude in any given set of circumstances, to choose one's own way."

Viktor Frankl

Sadly, this myth is true. If you choose to believe that your life is unfair, you will find it hard to be happy, because you are telling yourself that you are powerless and that life has made you a victim of circumstance. In giving away your power in such a way, the danger is that you are also giving away your sense of self.

But as Viktor Frankl observes in his remarkable book, *Man's Search for Meaning*, even in the most dire of circumstances it is still possible to choose your attitude to your situation and retain your sense of identity.

When a life is rocked by a series of misfortunes or tragedies, it is inevitable that the person who is suffering will cry out to themselves, "Why me?" It is only human, and necessary, to come to terms with what's happening. But beware of becoming trapped by a sense of personal injustice that will prevent you from moving on.

CHOOSING THE BRIGHT SIDE

The most powerful way to transform a sense of helplessness is to make a plan and take control; or to gain insight by focusing on other people's needs instead. Offering kindness to others can be a powerful way to redress the balance and change perspective.

Choosing to look on the bright side may sound like a platitude—and may seem difficult to achieve—but the new and brighter moments are usually there, and always worth the hunt. The path to happiness lies in our capacity to see the bigger picture, through positivity, hope, and compassion for others.

> Even in the most dire of circumstances it is still possible to choose your attitude to your situation and retain your sense of identity.

Everyone Deserves Happiness

At the heart of the five myths of happiness lies a deep-rooted fear that somehow happiness will remain elusive in your life. But that need not be so. Everyone deserves happiness—it is within everyone's grasp.

LETTING GO OF FEAR

"Happiness is a risk. If you're not a little scared, then you're not doing it right."

Sarah Addison Allen, *The Peach Keeper*

There are times in life when we need to risk all to gain happiness, while also letting go of some aspect that feels familiar. Strange as it may seem, sometimes the hardest thing to let go of is the safety blanket called fear. Fear encourages us to stay put, to remain risk-averse. It is the voice in your ear that tells you, "It's not worth the risk," and, "It's better not to try than to fail." By so not-doing, you are in danger of forfeiting the opportunity and living a life filled with regrets.

The pathways to happiness appear in many guises, and not all of them are immediately recognizable as ways you would want to venture down. They may look strange, too threatening, too full of obstacles, too far away from home, too frightening. But happiness is closely related to feelings of positive self-worth and achievement. We need to take calculated risks in order to grow and develop self-respect.

These key moments in life act as turning points that encourage us to take stock because there is a choice to be made, or something is about to change, and nothing will ever be the same again. It may be a milestone of achievement; a birthday that marks a new decade; a moment of loss and grief; or an opportunity that is simultaneously exciting and terrifying.

In these moments, we measure where we are against where we expected to be, and compare what we have achieved with what we originally dreamed of for ourselves. They are brave moments that challenge contentment and shake up the future.

> **Sometimes the hardest thing to let go of is the safety blanket called fear.**

Happiness is a large emotion, full of life. It doesn't thrive in situations where over-thinking stifles action, or where resentment and disappointment close the heart to the possibility of feeling joy. Somewhere between lost dreams and reality are thoughts you can dwell upon, steps you can take, and choices you can make that will dispel unwanted fears and turn potential regrets into opportunities for growth and change.

FEAR BUSTERS

The roots of fear lie in the mind and in our memory. Fear is the body's way of protecting us from real or perceived threat. Anxiety triggers the adrenaline response and increases blood flow to the heart, in preparation for "fight" or "flight." The Happiness Habit helps you to identify your thought triggers, so you can get to the source of the fear— and understand what makes you truly happy. Ask yourself:

* What are you frightened of? Is it a fear of something real, or something imaginary. (The mind cannot differentiate between the two.)

* What is motivating you to act and what might be holding you back?

* What do you have control over—so you can change it?

* What do you have no control over—so you will have to accept it?

* On a scale of 0 to 10, how happy will your decision make you?

* Will your decision lead you to step toward or away from further happiness?

Going With Flow

Much has been written about the "comfort" zone—that familiar space we operate within from day to day; and the "stretch" zone—where we learn new skills and develop new competencies. With competence comes confidence, which boosts self-worth and self-esteem. Coach and trainer Bev James often reminds those who attend her courses that unless we find the courage to step into the stretch zone, we will be forever wondering what life might have held, if only we had been a little braver.

"When people restrain themselves out of fear, their lives are by necessity diminished. Only through freely chosen discipline can life be enjoyed and still kept within the bounds of reason."

Mihaly Csíkszentmihályi

Mihaly Csíkszentmihályi (pronounced Me-Hi CheekSENTme-Hi-e) has had a huge influence on our understanding of what it means to be happy through his work on a concept he calls "Flow." He is one of the world's leading experts in the field of positive psychology. When we are in flow, we stop feeling conscious of time because we are so absorbed in the task. The results of our work seem to come through us rather than from us.

Csíkszentmihályi has identified the conditions that are needed for flow, which include:

❋ A sense of being involved in the task.

❋ A feeling of being outside the bounds of everyday reality.

❋ A sense of clarity and focus—we know what we are doing and where we are going.

❋ Taking on tasks that we have the skill level to complete.

❋ Having the discipline to concentrate on what we are doing.

❋ A sense of timelessness—of being so involved that we are not aware of time passing.

His work has clarified that for a task to be satisfying, it needs to be challenging, but within the scope of our abilities. If there is too much stress involved, productivity diminishes; if it is too easy, the motivation to do the task drops. Flow is the opposite of apathy—it drives us to act with purpose. When we are in flow, our sense of self is suspended, although completion of the task reaffirms self-value and provides a sense of satisfaction for work well done.

CHAPTER 2

THE HEALING POWER OF HAPPINESS

THE SCIENCE OF HAPPINESS

"Happiness is like a butterfly; the more you chase it, the more it will elude you, but if you turn your attention to other things, it will come and sit softly on your shoulder."

Buddhist proverb

Scientists have finally proved it—happiness is good for you. Those who are happy or have an optimistic and positive outlook are far less likely to suffer from clinical depression.

Studies of the effects of happiness have an impressive pedigree. Aristotle pondered the causes and impact of happiness as long ago as 322 BC. He suggested that the pursuit of happiness was an essential part of being human, and a goal in itself. More recently, scientists have discovered something that they call the "Happiness Paradox"—the more intent you are on pursuing solely your own path of happiness, the less likely you are to feel happy; whereas the more willing you are to focus on and help other people with no thought of your own gain, the happier and more content you will be.

There is another paradox: even though the standard of living has increased in most western countries over the past 30 years, national levels of happiness have not increased at all.

THE FORMULA FOR HAPPINESS

In the early 1970s, 34 percent of people in the UK described themselves as "very happy." By the late 1990s, at a time when the country's economy was buoyant, the figure had dropped 4 percent. The improved standard of living across the country appears to have had a slightly negative effect on the nation's happiness.

We are not quite as neighborly as we used to be, with 43 percent saying that neighbors are now less friendly than they were ten years ago. But overall, we are a pretty contented bunch. A Happiness Formula poll found, in 2005, that 92 percent of people described themselves as either fairly happy or very happy. Only 8 percent said they were fairly or very unhappy; and over 60 percent spoke to up to five friends each week.

It seems that the happiest country in the world is Switzerland, followed by Denmark, Sweden, Ireland, and the USA. Britain comes eighth.

On the one hand, the statistics are interesting and provide food for thought; they make up future government policies and social science surveys. On the other hand it feels slightly absurd to think that happiness can be measured and verified. Surely there cannot be a completely reliable way to measure people's feelings?

It is encouraging to know that governments around the world are now setting policies that factor in the importance of happiness, but at the end of the day, no matter what the statistics say, each individual in every house, street, college and office has the power to determine the collective optimism of a nation as a whole.

Bhutan—a Nation Built on Gross National Happiness (GNH)

High in the Himalayan mountains, nestled between the borders of India and China, lies the Buddhist kingdom of Bhutan. It is not a wealthy country, and it has a range of social and economic problems, but the people have been described as the happiest in the world. This is partially due to the influence of the fourth king of Bhutan, Jigme Singye Wangchuck, who came to believe that a country should be measured not only by economic success, but also by the level of contentment of its people. He travelled widely and was attending a conference in Havana when a journalist from India asked him about Bhutan's Gross National Product (GNP). The monarch is reported to have replied, "In Bhutan, we don't care about Gross National Product, we care about Gross National Happiness."

He went on to establish GNH as official government policy. It aims to balance spiritual and material care in the areas of social development, cultural preservation, conservation, and good governance. The Bhutanese people now have free health care and free education. Since the scheme was launched in 1978, life expectancy has increased by 20 years and household income per capita by 450 percent. Happiness really is something to smile about in Bhutan.

How to Have a Happy Planet

"Don't aim at success—the more you aim at it and make it a target, the more you are going to miss it. For success, like happiness, cannot be pursued; it must ensue ... as the unintended side-effect of one's personal dedication to a cause greater than oneself."

Viktor Frankl

The New Economics Foundation recommends five happy things to do each day to keep your happiness quotient healthy. It is the happy equivalent of eating your greens:

* Connect with those around you, and recognize the people in your life who are the cornerstones of your well-being.

* Be active. Find a form of movement and exercise that you enjoy and do it regularly—go for a walk, spend time outside.

* Pay attention to the world around you and the beauty that surrounds you.

* Keep learning. Take up a new subject; rediscover an old passion; repair your bike; sign up for a course; learn a musical instrument.

* Give your time, money, warmth, a smile, a gift, friendship—anything that will add to other people's lives and help to motivate them to do the same.

The Foundation has also devised an innovative method of measurement that assesses the connection between ecological efficiency and well-being around the world, and assesses results, country by country. Known as the Happy Planet Index, it uses data based upon life expectancy, experiences of well-being, and the ecological footprint of each country.

The results show that consuming high levels of natural resources does not result in high levels of well-being. Results from the 2012 edition of the Happy Planet Index show that just nine countries in the world are achieving high levels of sustainability and well-being. Eight of those countries are in South America and the Caribbean.

The scores of high-income countries are considerably reduced by their large ecological footprints. The USA is in position 105 out of 151 countries. New Zealand is the highest scoring western nation, in 28th place.

Scientists have finally proved it—
happiness is good for you.

LOVE MATTERS

"Touch has a memory."
John Keats

Scientists tell us that the roots of self-esteem stem from the earliest stages of our life. According to Sue Gerhardt, author of *Why Love Matters*, the unconditional love that we receive as babies appears to influence brain development. Babies who are comforted when they cry learn to soothe themselves as they grow; whereas babies who are left to cry develop a highly sensitized response to stress, which means that they find it harder to manage stress when they are adults.

But why is this? When we are stressed or feel in danger, the body produces a hormone called cortisol. We need a certain amount of cortisol, but in high stress situations, we produce too much, too often, which can have a tiring effect on the body and leave people less able to manage their emotions. Those who are highly sensitive to stress will try to self-soothe—for example, by eating high carbohydrate foods.

A HUG A DAY HELPS
YOU WORK, REST, AND PLAY

The good news is that getting physical with someone else will reduce your stress levels, reduce your cortisol levels, and increase the production of oxytocin, a "happy" hormone, in the body. All of this will make you feel happier, and will also boost your immune system.

**Don't worry about the science behind the results,
just make a mental note to:**

✳ Hug a friend ✳ Get a massage ✳ Comfort a baby
✳ Hold hands with your loved one ✳ Stroke the dog
✳ Cuddle the cat ✳ Make love ✳ Go dancing
✳ Be more physical

The more we are in touch (literally) with one another, the calmer, happier, and healthier we are.

SHAPE UP FOR HAPPINESS

"Happiness not only feels good but it's good for you. We know that happy people on average have better health. Happy people live longer. Happy people have more friendships and are more likely to give money to charity."

Ed Diener (Dr Happy)

What if, instead of going to the gym to exercise, we were going to the gym to become happier? What if, instead of running on the treadmill to lose weight, we were told that running on the treadmill would improve our friendships? Would it help increase membership numbers? It would be good to think so.

Exercise generates happiness, firstly, by making us feel more healthy and energetic. It can also be team-based and competitive, which appeals to those whose achievements affect their happiness levels. Secondly, it triggers physiological changes within the body and the release of "happy hormones."

Science tells us that those people who exercise at least two or three times per week experience significantly less depression, anger, and stress than those who exercise less frequently or not at all.

> ✳ If you are feeling a bit low, a quick 20-minute burst of exercise can change your mood and raise your happiness levels.

* Those who do battle with depression are encouraged to exercise for 30 minutes per day for a minimum of 3–5 days each week.

* I once worked with a highly successful entrepreneur who said she was caught doing star jumps in an office corridor while waiting for an interview. It was her favorite way to overcome anxiety.

The Cochrane Review is the most influential review of its kind in the world. It has produced an analysis of 23 studies on exercise and depression. Their results showed unequivocally the impact that exercise has on lowering the incidence of depression. Exercise was shown to be as effective as antidepressant medication in helping to reduce mental symptoms.

Controversy remains about whether exercise leads to improved mental well-being, or whether those with positive mental well-being are more likely to exercise—but for anyone non-medical, the message is the same: Exercise makes you happier.

Easy ways to shape up for happiness:
* Get on your bike! * Dance yourself happy.
* Smile while you walk. * Run round the block.
* Take the stairs, not the lift.

Don't worry about how much exercise you take—just choose to begin.

HOW TO MOTIVATE YOURSELF TO EXERCISE

The world tends to be divided between those who love to exercise—and those who prefer to talk about why they should exercise. When you still have your exercise 'Learner' plates on, short-term goals that include the 'happy factor' are more motivating than long-term goals. For example, telling yourself, "It's a beautiful day for a walk and the fresh air will clear my head"; is more motivating than "I must go for a run round the block, it will lower my cholesterol."

* "I want to feel more energetic and upbeat." Try setting the alarm 15 minutes earlier and go for a quick walk around the block. You will feel more positive from the beginning of the day.

* "I want to feel calmer and happier." If you are feeling uptight or angry, exercise will help to release tension.

> **What if, instead of going to the gym to exercise, we were going to the gym to become happier?**

* "I feel overwhelmed by my problems." Many people, including business leaders and politicians, go walking or running when they have to think through a problem.

* "I want to lose weight and look great." Many people lose weight through exercise rather than going on a diet.

* "I want to look younger." Exercise keeps the blood healthy and helps the skin to renew and replenish old cells. It will help you sleep better too, all of which adds up to a more youthful and energetic you.

* "But I hate exercise." Hating exercise is like saying you hate being able to move your arms and legs. Exercise is easy. It is what we were designed to do. You just need to keep increasing the amount and speed you move your body, each day.

THE SPIRIT OF HAPPINESS

"My main commitment is... to achieve a happy, successful life...
for a happy, successful life, much depends on our
mental attitude, our mental outlook."

The Dalai Lama

Happiness is essential to our spiritual well-being, and a relationship exists between levels of happiness and involvement in spiritual practice.

The path to spiritual happiness has nothing to do with material gains, and everything to do with seeking inner peace and understanding. In prayer, or contemplation, or meditation, a primary goal is to let go of negativity and attachment to emotions that prevent us from feeling compassionate toward one another—and ourselves.

All forms of spiritual practice and religion emphasize a connection between spiritual fulfillment and happiness. The ability to overcome and control our human cravings, in whatever form that temptation takes, is a key part of the process of learning on the path to fulfillment. There is another common theme, too—the quest for the happiness and well-being of all our fellow humans. In all churches, mosques, and temples of the world, happiness is a blessed state that cannot be completely experienced in this earthly life, but can be strived for, to achieve in the next.

Just as the repetition of positive thoughts will reprogram the neural pathways of the mind to think more positively, so, too, the spiritual rituals of happiness have been used over centuries to fine-tune the mind—and the heart. The process of prayer in all its forms opens us up to the possibility of Universal love and awakens us to our greater purpose.

Spiritual teachings include the concept of forgiveness, because only by finding a way to forgive ourselves and others can we learn from our mistakes and develop and grow as human beings. Earthly happiness is less than perfect; all spiritual traditions share the belief that the ultimate state of bliss will be attained in the next life rather than this one.

Ask the Universe

"At the moment of commitment the entire Universe conspires to assist you."

Johann Wolfgang von Goethe

Who has not at some point in their lives been struck by an extraordinary coincidence that has transformed their life? One second you are making a wish and the next second the opportunity is there in front of you, as if by magic. These are the moments where the idea of guardian angels feels tangible and it feels as if the Universe is very much taking care of our needs. "Be careful what you wish for," friends might say, or "Ask, and the Universe will provide."

Many people hold an instinctive belief that if we focus with good heart and are clear about what we want to achieve we can manifest our own reality. This process has been called many things over the centuries: it is one of the functions of prayer, it is commonly referred to as the law of attraction, and has more controversially been termed the "cosmic ordering service."

The popular German author Bärbel Mohr was the first to coin the phrase "cosmic ordering," the idea being that if we focus fully on the things that we want in life, they will appear and our fortunes can change. The law of attraction, similarly, focuses on the power of our thinking. If we see things in a negative light, we will attract negativity into our world. On the other hand, if we project a very precise and positive vision of what we would like our future to be like, the Universe will conspire to help to make this happen. The idea that we can influence outcomes with the power of our thought is seductive—provided we use such influence for the common good.

DEVELOPING A
HAPPY BRAIN

"Neurons that fire together, wire together."
Donald Hebb

We know very little about the human brain—or more accurately, an extremely small percentage of people in the world, who have trained as neuroscientists, know a great deal about the brain in comparison with the rest of us. In fact, their understanding has doubled in the last 20 years, but by their own admission, the brain remains the last frontier of the human body.

Interestingly, every new discovery seems to find more evidence of the brain's plasticity; its ability to adapt and reinvent itself over time. Playing an important role in this is the front area of the brain, known as the prefrontal cortex. This is a uniquely human feature. It allows us to develop free choice, helps us to develop a sense of right or wrong, helps us to regulate our emotions, and it is a large part of who we are.

What has all this got to do with

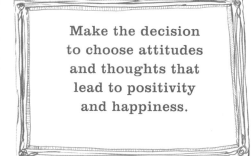

Make the decision to choose attitudes and thoughts that lead to positivity and happiness.

happiness? The brain is changing all the time and as we change our mind, so we strengthen or weaken the connections between the cells in the brain known as neurons. The neurons send messages along pathways. The more we repeat a thought, whether positive or negative, happy or sad, the stronger the pathway becomes.

Our thoughts, like most people, prefer to take shortcuts. It is rather like cutting a corner across a grass verge. The first time someone does it, barely a footprint is left on the grass, but if everyone else takes the shortcut too, it won't be long before a new pathway has been forged.

> **Even in the direst circumstances it is still possible to choose your attitude to your situation and retain your sense of identity.**

Love, too, stimulates the brain in a positive way.

A greater level of brain activity in the left side of the prefrontal cortex is associated with positive emotion and wellbeing. This side of the brain puts the brakes on negative thinking. So if you practice positive thinking on a regular basis, the neural pathways in the brain that are associated with positivity will strengthen.

The flow of various neurochemicals in the brain varies from time to time. Interestingly, when people practice gratitude in a conscious way, the levels of reward-based "happy" hormones, such as dopamine, are increased.

Love, too, stimulates the brain in a positive way. Someone in love only needs to look at a picture of their loved one for the parts of the brain associated with positivity and rewards to become more active.

There is now evidence to show that where we focus our attention can consciously change the way we think. If we draw our attention to all the things that make us mad and angry and unhappy, and hang on to those thoughts, we will strengthen their power. If, on the other hand, we choose to reframe the negative into something positive, or focus consciously on positive and happy memories, then those are the neurons that are going to be strengthened.

Those in the field of alternative health have known about this for years, but now there is proof in a form that conforms with the traditional medical way of testing.

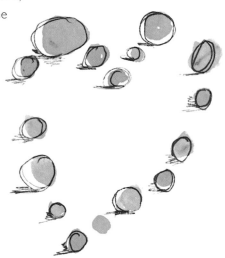

USE IT OR LOSE IT

As we get older, we gradually shed some of our brain cells in a process that is known as "cortical thinning." By the time we are 80 years old, we will have lost approximately 4 percent of our total number of brain cells. However, it seems that the brain, like the rest of the body, benefits from exercise. In one scientific study the brains of meditators and non-meditators were compared, at the same age. Those who meditated on a regular basis had less cortical thinning.

Think of happiness as a bottomless pot of joy, talent, hope, and gratitude. The more you use it; the more you give to others, the further you spread its contents—the happier you will feel. Using our capacity for compassion and kindness strengthens our energy for living and our joy for life. The pot will continue to remain filled to the brim. If you disregard your pot of happiness, it will begin to evaporate. The less you use, the more you try to conserve only for yourself, the more anger, resentment, and gloom enters the pot—the faster happiness will fade away.

How Many Ways Have You Laughed Lately?

According to journalist Nick Harding, the 40 million speakers of Marathi in India use at least eight different words to describe laughter.

Khudukhudu: The soft giggles of a young child

Phidiphid: Raucous laughter

Hyahya: Polite laughter

Khadakhada: Children laughing loudly

Khaskhas: Mild chuckles

Khokho: Laughter that is loud and rowdy

Khikhi: Laughing like a horse

Phisphis: Mocking or disparaging laughter

KNOW THE SYMPTOMS

"None but ourselves can free our minds."

Bob Marley

The symptoms of happiness are easy to spot and they are contagious. Children especially are liable to catch a bout of happiness very quickly and take great delight in passing it on.

Cries of laughter; big smiles, the desire to run, jump, shout, and try new things are all symptomatic of the joyous impact of being happy. It may not last for very long, but it is powerful and fun while it lasts.

The symptoms of being less than happy are also contagious. They take hold more slowly, but may last for longer and show up in many ways. It is wise to try to immunize yourself against the power of negative thoughts before you are exposed to them; or to boost your levels of positive thinking if you know you have come into contact with them.

The common signs of chronic negativity are:

Reproachfulness. You may blame yourself, your family, your job, your circumstances, for the way you are feeling about yourself and about your life.

Regret. You may have a general sense of sadness; suffer feelings of worry and loneliness; feel unlovable, let down, or generally disappointed with life, your friends, or your achievements.

Anxiety. You may feel overstretched, worried or worn down by responsibilities and the demands of others.

> It is wise to try to immunize yourself against the power of negative thoughts before you are exposed to them.

Self-defeating behavior. You may be snappy and bad-tempered, feel a lack of personal motivation, and have a history of overeating, smoking, or drinking too much, or taking too little exercise; then feel sorry for yourself because of health problems or financial worries.

Becoming isolated. Everyone has personal demons and self-destructive habits that jeopardize happiness from time to time; people tend to tuck themselves away when they are unhappy. Those negative feelings and behaviors can also be flags of distress, signalling "help me" while simultaneously pushing away the very people who care about you.

Premature aging. Discontent and unhappiness show up on the body. Unhappy people slump more; they seem to have more wrinkle lines, from frowning so much; they may neglect their appearance, so hair, teeth, nails, and clothes look tired.

Becoming Happy

The good news is that you don't have to be happy to become happy. The moment you begin to smile, laugh, relax your shoulders, and wipe away the furrowed brow, two interesting things happen:

* The brain responds by releasing endorphins, which are the attraction hormones, and oxytocin—the "cuddle" hormone—making you feel instantly more positive, relaxed, and attractive.

* Those around you will behave more positively.

The result is that the brain learns to become happy, even if you didn't feel that way to begin with. The other secrets of happiness can be easily learned, too. Practising them over time will see you through tougher times and carry others with you.

CHAPTER 3

THE BARRIERS
TO HAPPINESS

REMOVING BARRIERS

"Very little is needed to make a happy life; it is all within yourself in your way of thinking."

Marcus Aurelius

Much has been written about the power of positive thinking and the way it can help areas of the brain literally to rewire over a period of time; but for positive thinking to become a new habit, you first need to let go of the negative thoughts that may have become a mainstay of getting by, up until now.

Our moans, groans, and grumbles may seem very innocent individually. If they have become an ingrained habit, you may not even realize that they are there, but their impact over a long period can be devastating. Negative thoughts train your brain to think negatively. These thoughts will affect your choices and your actions, and their outcomes, because they have an impact on the way you see the world. Over time, they have the power to steal the potential for joy in life because they stir up envy and discontent and it begins to feel as if other people must be living a more fulfilled life, or having more fun. For some, this habit can lead to depression because the way we think influences the chemistry of the body. Our capacity for resilience and our physical well-being suffer.

This section of the book offers strategies for removing the barriers to happiness that you may have inadvertently set in your path. Few of them are as impassable as they appear. All of them are easy to go over, under, or around, once you understand them and can see why they are there. The power tools of success are self-awareness, positive thinking, practice, and persistence—which are valuable additions to your happiness toolbox.

IN ELEMENT

"[The]Element—the place where the things you love to do and the things you are good at come together."
Sir Ken Robinson

How happy are you in your work? Do you love what you do or is it simply a means to an end? Is there a boundary in your life between your time working and your time of leisure, or is there a seamless continuation, where work and play are one and the same. Does your work fire you up with enthusiasm, or drain your energy? The process of loving what you do and doing what you love is what Ken Robinson calls being in your element.

Ken Robinson is passionate about the importance of creativity in our education systems and in our personal development. He has a heartfelt belief that we each have unique talents and abilities that can inspire us to achieve much more than we currently dream possible. But in order to find out what those talents are, we need to tune into the world of our imagination, our intuition, and our senses, to truly experience and be stimulated by the world.

> **The power tools of success are self-awareness, positive thinking, practice, and persistence—which together will become the happiness habit.**

We also need to let go of self-limiting ideas of what we can't do or are not good at. Many of these attitudes stem back to our school days where the pathway through exams inevitably led to most of us focusing on what we were good at, rather than on the things we most loved. The route to finding your element includes letting go of any preconceptions about what your skills and talents might be and to open your mind to new experiences and opportunities. We never lose our capacity to learn, grow, and change, and we deserve to find happiness in our work—and to find work that we love to do.

Clear The Happiness Barriers

The barriers to personal happiness are often the same barriers that block effective communication. So often we think we are paying attention, or making ourselves understood, when the opposite is true. Here are ten ways to communicate with very few words, but genuine engagement.

Making someone feel acknowledged, heard, and respected is the greatest gift of happiness that can ever be bestowed. As the good saying goes: you have one mouth and two ears—make sure you listen twice as much as you speak!

✳ Smile

✳ Communicate with your eyes

✳ Show your enthusiasm

✳ Engage with interest

✳ Put your cell phone on mute

✳ Pay full attention

✳ Be sincere ✳ Respect differences

✳ Simply LISTEN ✳ Show gratitude

Choose to Feel Happy

"I want a life that sizzles and pops and makes me laugh out loud."

Shauna Niequist

Barry Neil Kaufman (known as "Bears") is founder of the Option Institute in Massachussetts; his work in the field of happiness is respected and renowned worldwide. In his book Happiness is a Choice, *he observed his clients and others over a period of years to see whether he could discover what made some people more likely to be happy than others. For those who want to know more, his book is a warm and encouraging read. In the book, he identifies six happiness "shortcuts" (the word is offered tongue-in-cheek) which I paraphrase here:*

1. Make happiness your priority. How many of us complain about being unhappy without taking steps to change our situation? How many of us talk about what it would take to be happy without putting those actions at the top of our "to do" list?

2. Choose to be your authentic self. Many people are afraid to be themselves; they wear a mask to cover up their true feelings and worry about how to behave. When we drop the mask, we become less afraid because we become true to ourselves and accept ourselves for who we are.

3. Let go of judgments. When we hold on to fixed beliefs about ourselves, events, or other people, we prevent ourselves from opening our minds to a different view.

4. Be present. Being present lies at the heart of meditation practice. Kaufman adds to this the conundrum that "Unhappiness does not exist in the present moment." We become unhappy only when we judge events retrospectively or anticipate their outcome.

5. Be grateful. When we are grateful, we become happier; when we are happy, we become more grateful.

6. Decide to be happy. This is the most effective shortcut of all.

PRACTICE THE HAPPINESS HABIT

*There are many easy ways to develop the happiness habit.
Here are a few instant mood switchers that can be used
when groans and grumbles threaten to chase away the
chance of happiness on a daily basis:*

* **Watch your language.** The moment you hear yourself think or say passive words, such as I wish, should, might, can't, swap them for more active words, such as, I can, I will, I am. You will feel instantly happier if your choice of language puts you in control of your life.

* **Learn to say no.** Busy people tend to say yes to things just because they can. Unassertive people tend to say yes to things because they can't quite manage to say no. A simple sentence, such as, "I won't be able to do that for you because I am already very busy/fully committed/doing something else," will get you out of trouble.

* **Awaken your senses.** Your senses send messages to the brain. When your senses are alert, you feel more alive. Focus fully on what you are doing at every moment of the day. There is joy to be had in every task: the sight of a robin hopping about while you are weeding; the smell of the ingredients while you are baking; the sound of your

children chattering while discovering their world; the hug or touch of a friend or lover. Appreciating the small things awakens awareness of the bigger things, and helps to put us back in touch with our true selves.

* **Relax, breathe, stand up straight.** The body holds tension. When we feel anxious, our breathing becomes shallow and our shoulders rise. By taking deep breaths and shaking out the shoulders, you will release tension, improve your posture, and immediately feel lighter and happier.

* **Look after your body.** Make time to have a soak in the bath, or a steaming power shower; keep your hair trimmed; wear your favorite shirt; massage your skin. The skin is the largest organ of the body. It needs oxygen and nutrients to keep healthy and keep you protected. If you feel good physically, you will feel better mentally. Get enough sleep. It is hard to feel happy if you are exhausted.

* **Laugh**. Do you remember what it feels like to shake with uncontrollable laughter; to feel consumed by the joy of a single moment, shared with someone you care about or can have fun with? Laughter wipes away tension in a single breath and turns a frowning face into one that is alive and beautiful. It doesn't take much to trigger a giggle: just thinking about something

funny that has happened in the past can provoke laughter and increase happiness. Phone a friend, tell a silly joke, read a favorite cartoon strip, look for the absurd in every situation. Laugh—several times a day.

* **Smile.** Smiling draws people toward you. It is a gift of positive intention. When you smile at someone, you make them feel welcome and good about themselves. One person's happiness can lighten the mood of a whole roomful of people. As the saying goes, "A smile is contagious—pass it on!"

* **Be kind to others.** Studies have proven again and again that the quickest and most satisfying route to finding happiness is not to think about yourself all the time but to focus on other people and what they need instead. As human beings we are social creatures who like to be connected to one another. Giving and gratitude are essential ingredients in the formulation and experience of happiness.

* **Listen.** When we tune in to what people are really saying, we feel more strongly connected and more compassionate. When we feel heard and understood we feel more loved, better supported, more contented, and we are more likely to listen to and help others.

MUSTN'T GRUMBLE

"The present moment is filled with joy and happiness. If you are attentive, you will see it."

Thich Nhat Hanh

When someone says, "Hi. How are you?" what do you reply? It probably depends on your age, your nationality, how well you know the person, and your frame of mind. Often the question is more an extension of "Hello" rather than a genuine enquiry into the state of someone's health. Occasionally, people will take the enquiry literally (usually when you are in a tearing hurry) and spend the next half-hour offering a blow by blow account of their latest medical history. (Well, you did ask …) But commonly there will be a long-suffering sigh followed by, "I'm fine," "Mustn't grumble," 'Bearing up," "Surviving," or some such phrase. What does that really mean? Would people say that if they were truly happy? Probably not. Would people feel happier if they said instead, "I'm great thank you; never better!" The chances are, they might.

It usually takes no more effort to think a cheery thought than it does a gloomy

> It usually takes no more effort to think a cheery thought than it does a gloomy one.

one, and yet many people spend less time being consciously happy and more time focused on grumbling—about the weather, the traffic, the lack of parking, their boss, their partner, their lack of finances, their children.

The grumble habit is normal for many people, and it can be insidious. The more you complain, the more you notice to complain about, and then others around you start to grouse, too. Conversations become a grumblefest of grumble one-upmanship. "You think *you* had a terrible time on your vacation, just let me tell you about what happened to *us* …" "I know just what you mean, I had the same problem the other day …" "The government is terrible," "The town has changed," "Things used to be so much better." And so it goes on …

Happy people are less likely to grumble. They tend to notice the good in things first, and welcome the opportunity rather than notice its failings. They "choose to do" things rather than "decide not to do" things. Grumblers tend to look for faults, whereas happy people accept, or adapt.

RESET YOUR GRUMBLE POSITIONING SYSTEM

Try to listen to yourself talking in the same way you would listen to a GPS system. Imagine what it would be like to have a grumbling GPS while on the vacation of a lifetime. The sun is out, you are feeling relaxed, the car is packed, and you are ready to explore new territory. But every time you reach a road junction or turn a corner there is a complaint, a sigh, or an expression of regret from your Grumble Positioning System. "What a shame you didn't go left there;" "This junction is always a pain;" "I get so tired of being stuck in traffic;" "The café we passed an hour ago was so much nicer than the one you are stopping at." Your mood would sink; your enjoyment would plummet. You would probably turn it off and go back to map reading.

If when you speak you tend to put a dampener on things, you may find that people tune out from what you say and may even avoid your company. Try instead to say something positive first, before the negativity kicks in. Laugh at the things that annoy you and try to see the possibility instead of the problem. The chances are that those you are talking to will follow your lead and echo your mood with a positive reply.

Happiness embraces opportunity and praises achievement. It creates an environment where better things become possible and joy is appreciated. Swap your Grumbling Positioning System for one that is grateful and you will start to see things differently and immediately feel happier.

DON'T PROCRASTINATE

"Only put off until tomorrow, what you are willing to die having left undone."

Pablo Picasso

Procrastination is the thief of time—and it will steal your life, too, given half a chance. Procrastination is a major enemy of happiness because it will never allow you to plan ahead with confidence, relax without guilt, or produce your best work. Procrastinators miss out on parties, vacations, tax breaks, and even having children, because their dread of deadlines means they haven't been paying enough attention to how they prioritize their time. The art of chronic delay is worry dressed up as fear and accessorized with avoidance, pain, and guilt. Any pleasures in the life of a procrastinator feel stolen surreptitiously, because wherever you are and whatever you are doing, you know you should really be somewhere different, doing something else instead.

> **A well-planned schedule can become a thing of joy and a route to happiness.**

Chronic procrastinators feel full of self-loathing because they know they disrupt other people's lives with their delays. In letting others down, they let themselves down.

Whatever the original cause (and there are many different reasons,) the underlying problem is the strong belief that they can never be anywhere or get anything done on time. Of course, that is far from the truth.

Many procrastinators seek their pleasures in gratuitous diversions. Drawers will be tidied efficiently at the moment they should be getting dressed for work; crossword puzzles are completed at the moment a letter should be written; someone else's problem is solved at the very moment they should be prioritizing their own. A common problem for a procrastinator is the inability to say no. Another is having an unrealistic idea of how much they can achieve in a day. But the greatest one of all is a misplaced belief that they are hopeless, and the consequent tendency to focus more on their fear of the finish date while paying no proper attention on when or how to start.

START NOW

"To do" lists are torture for a procrastinator, because they seem to get longer and longer every day, but a well-planned schedule can become a thing of joy and a route to happiness:

❋ Buy or print a one-page year planner so you can easily count the weeks and days throughout the year at a glance.

* Look around your home or your place of work, and make a list of all the things that you have started, but not finished. If you feel yourself procrastinating at the very thought of starting, just write down one thing. If you are serious in your quest for happiness, choose to do this now.

* Next think about when you would like (or when you need) to have completed this task. Circle the date on your year planner.

* Work backward in your mind through the various tasks and stages that you will need to complete in order to achieve your end goal. Think about this in stages, according to the complexity of the task. Think of a realistic time span for each completion stage, and then repeat the exercise, doubling the amount of time you initially thought was necessary to complete each one.

* The chances are, if you have already been procrastinating, that the date you come up with was some days or weeks earlier than today's date, telling you that you should have started by now and you are behind already. Normally, you would panic at this point and choose to do something else, as a diversion. Instead, tell yourself that you now have three choices: to arrange to extend the deadline; to ask someone to help you to deliver on time; or both. Sticking your head in the sand and pretending that time is malleable is no longer an option—because it isn't.

* The final step is to create a schedule—preferably using color to bring it to life. It will be best to devise your own layout, in a way that matches the needs of your task and the way you think.

* Draw it, create it in Excel, but map it out in such a way that you can pin the printed-out version on your wall and see it all the time. Set up reminders in your online diary if it helps—but the trick is to have something in front of you as a visual reminder of what actions to take at every moment of every day.

Two important points are worth bearing in mind. First, DO NOT use the actual deadline as your scheduled deadline. Make sure the deadline that you list on your schedule is a good two weeks (or more) ahead of the formal cut-off. This is the golden rule. If necessary, leave the real date off your schedule altogether, so your brain is not distracted by it.

Rule number two is to highlight your START dates in a brighter color than your finish date, and tick them off as you go. Most schedules are focused around completion dates, which for the procrastinator is no use at all.

Once you discover the joy of completing tasks in good time or on time, your belief in yourself will slowly change—and you will have time to be happy on your own terms, too.

Heed the Happiness Project

"As much as we try to find the Bluebird of Happiness, we're also plagued by the Pigeons of Discontent."

Gretchen Rubin

When I stumbled upon Gretchen Rubin's concept of the pigeons of discontent, I laughed out loud. As founder of the Happiness Project, she has created a series of practical tips and strategies to help people to reframe common obstacles to happiness. Her philosophy is that the pigeons of discontent often get in the way of our search for happiness, but many problems can be overcome with simple and practical strategies, and by consciously changing our habits.

Another happiness guru who also focuses on the concept of discontent and disappointment is Dan Gilbert, Professor of Psychology at Harvard University. He challenges the accepted view that having choice makes us happy, and argues that, for the vast majority, having the option to change our minds can make us fretful and dissatisfied.

In an experiment that he has repeated many times, he asks

individuals to rank seven Monet paintings in order of personal preference from 1 to 7. He then tells participants that he would like to give them a print as a memento, but he can only offer copies of the prints that the person has ranked third and fourth. He asks everyone to rank the same images over again. The favorite image remains in first place, but the chosen "souvenir" print moves up to second place, while the rejected print moves down to sixth place. Even though the participants had no real preference for the souvenir image at the outset, by the end of the experiment they have developed a false preference for the painting.

> **The trick is to have something in front of you as a visual reminder at every moment of every day.**

Human beings seem to like clarity in their pursuit of happiness.

GOODBYE TO COMPLACENCY

"Remember this—if you are in a position to take things for granted, you are already blessed beyond your needs."
Andrew Bienkowski

Many of us don't realize how happy we are because we take our current life so much for granted. We are always looking for faults and wishing for something else. Familiarity and routine threaten the specialness of what we have right now.

Most children and teenagers are blissfully complacent, especially those who have grown up with the material comforts of the western world. They take their education for granted; they expect to be fed; most will know that they are loved; and many will have clothes, gadgets, or vacations paid for by those who care for them. Children deserve to feel secure and safe until they are ready to make their own way in the world. It is part of the deal. Very often it is not until children have left home for the first time, or started families themselves, that their sense of appreciation really begins.

But if the pattern continues through life—getting without giving, receiving without reciprocation—both the

> **Many of us don't realize how happy we are because we take our current life so much for granted.**

giver and the receiver are left in a place of disadvantage. Complacency shows in a lack of awareness of others and an absence of gratitude. It is perfectly possible to have fun and be complacent at the same time in the short-term, but in the long-term, those who are complacent about their friendships, relationships, or material comforts without safeguarding them may lose them altogether.

Even those who have had a difficult life need to be alert to complacency. Being aware of what it feels like to be neglected or overlooked can help us to appreciate the value of care and kindness, and encourage us not to be complacent in learning how to treat others better than we are treated ourselves.

THE NATURE OF GRATITUDE

Thinking back through your life, is there anyone who has shown you support and care who you have forgotten to thank or acknowledge? Is there anyone in your life now, who is always there for you, to the point where you take them for granted? When you consider the path that your education and your career have taken, who has helped you along the way?

Say thank you for the small things. Saying thank you, especially for the things we receive as a matter of routine, each and every day, is the easiest and kindest way of making someone feel loved and appreciated. A spontaneous thank you, a big smile, plenty of eye contact and perhaps a hug can make the dullest chore the happiest task in the world.

Do something differently. Memory expert Tony Buzan says that the mind tends to remember things that are different, not things that are the same. So if your routine is unchanged day to day, you will begin to become complacent, because you will no longer notice what you are doing. Making the effort to do things differently occasionally, or swapping responsibilities, or saying thank you with a surprise gesture, will stay in the mind for a long time and have a great impact.

Give before you get. We don't need a reason to show someone we care about that we appreciate them. Be spontaneous and show someone how much you care before they have done anything for you.

Walk a mile in another man's shoes. Experiencing the world from another person's perspective is guaranteed to help us to understand them better. Actions are what create understanding.

WE ARE ALL CONNECTED

Doris Pilkington (Nugi Garimara) is an award-winning Australian writer of Aboriginal descent, best known internationally for her book *Follow the Rabbit-Proof Fence*, which was turned into an excellent film. I attended one of her talks a few years ago and was struck by her opening lines.

She told the audience that in Aboriginal culture, when you ask someone, "How are you today?" it is understood that you are enquiring not just about the person in front of you, but about their ancestors, too. The question is taken very seriously, because wellbeing does not relate solely to an individual. It relates to all the people connected to them in their family and in their community, to their environment, in its broadest sense, and to their past—because we are all connected and we have a shared history. The concept took my breath away.

When a question is asked with such sincerity, and the answer given with such perspective, it immediately has more meaning. "How. Are. You?" How can you ever ask the question lightly again?

Would everyone be happier if we all took the question more seriously; if we asked it in a way that tuned into people's true state of mind? Those who reply with a half-hearted, "I'm fine," are more often than not saying, "Actually, I'm not fine. I'm not too happy really and I would love it if someone had time to chat to me for a while."

If someone is unhappy, it is a reflection on those around them. Something is out of balance. In speaking to an unhappy person, you have a chance to influence their mood and make them feel connected once again. If the gift of listening is given to one person, they are more likely to pass it on to another.

The person who feels listened to, cared for, and supported is much more likely to reply, "I'm very well, thank you; great, actually," which allows you to say, "That's wonderful. I'm so glad—please tell me what's been happening in your life."

UNDERSTANDING ANGER

"For every minute you are angry you lose sixty seconds of happiness."
Ralph Waldo Emerson

Anger, rage, and resentment can be all-consuming. They are strong emotions that can take over the body, both physically and mentally. It is natural to feel irritated and angry from time to time, but the irony is that if we hold on to anger, or the feelings get out of control, it will wreak more damage upon us than the person or situation we are angry with.

When someone becomes angry, their blood pressure rises, their heart rate increases, and they may be moved either to tears of frustration or a burst of temper. When we are happy, there is a similar physical reaction—but the outcome is joy and laughter instead of temper. It is very difficult to feel anger and happiness at the same time.

The most effective weapon against anger is often humor because it has the power to alter one state of mind to another. That's why the child who is bullied in the playground so often becomes the clown, to get out of trouble; and why international diplomats often have the gift of wit and charm, to defuse difficult situations before they flare up.

When my younger brother and I were children, he used to drive me crazy. He didn't mean to—he was my kid brother, that's what they do. But as well as triggering my irritation, he also learned how to manage my response. If he saw me getting mad at him, he would start to laugh, and the madder I got the more he would laugh (a bit nervously perhaps, but determinedly nevertheless.) After a few moments his laughter would become infectious. It is very hard to keep a straight face when someone else is in stitches. Soon I would be laughing, too. The mood changed and whatever it was rarely seemed important any more.

Sometimes, of course, anger runs much deeper. It may be the result of suffering emotional pain or hurt; you may have been storing up grudges over a long period of time. It may become a deeply held rage that you don't want to let go of. Over time it becomes a part of who you are and may lead you toward feelings of depression. Denying it will drive it deeper, so that it comes out inappropriately at other times. It is hard to feel happy when you are carrying such a load.

THE POWER OF FORGIVENESS

The antidote to deeply held anger is forgiveness. It is the decision to let go of feelings of resentment, the choice to forgive the person who has hurt you—not necessarily to condone what they have done, although responsibility often rests with both sides, but to set yourself free from the grasp of the anger. It is not an easy thing to do. The other person may not be ready to change.

Some victims of violent crime describe having to repeat this process of forgiveness regularly, as the memories return and the feelings rise again. Those who succeed in finding it within themselves to forgive, say that they now have a chance of happiness again. With forgiveness comes a sense of peace and the sense that you can continue with your life.

It means committing to a process of change.

* Ask yourself, "Why am I hanging on to my anger? What value is it to me?"

* "What would happen if I exchanged my anger for forgiveness? How would I feel within myself?"

* Consider how the situation to date has affected you and whether you have become a victim of your anger because it has become a part of who you are.

* Focus on thinking about the person who has caused you hurt, and if possible consider their side of the story.

* See whether you can find it within yourself to forgive the person, even if you can't forgive their words or their actions.

You may need to repeat this process more than once, but in shifting your attention to letting go of anger you will gradually become free of the situation that is stealing a part of your life and happiness.

NAVIGATING GRIEF

"Smile, though your heart is breaking."
Nat King Cole

It may seem odd to have a section on grief in a book that is about the secrets of happiness, but the reality is that most of us will experience periods of grief in our lives, and sometimes we can get stuck there. We may have the sense that we no longer deserve to be happy because it would in some way be a betrayal of the sadness and depth of emotion we still feel. So this section is included to suggest that choosing happiness is not disrespectful to those we have lost, and it need not diminish the importance or the memory of what has passed. Happiness is the gift that others would wish us to have if they care about us—and the gift that we deserve if we care about ourselves.

The whole of life is about beginnings and endings, happiness and loss. It seems we can't live life to the full without experiencing both states; we can't enjoy one, without experiencing the other.

Coping with endings of any sort can be acutely painful. We first learn this in childhood. Perhaps you remember the pain of leaving

> The whole of life is about beginnings and endings, happiness and loss.

your neighborhood and friends because you were moving to a new place; maybe your family experienced the devastation of a divorce; perhaps a beloved pet died—or worse, you may have lost someone close to you. In adulthood we may experience love and the pain of break-up several times, and the impact can be devastating. The pain of losing a life partner after many years together may never go away.

Grief carries echoes, so every time we experience a new loss, we are reminded of the losses that have gone before. Sometimes this intensifies our sense of grief, but it may create a sense of numbness in those who choose to button down their feelings and to deny their pain, so afraid are they of the intensity of their feelings. The danger is that their denial or detachment may insulate them from future happiness as well.

THE ART OF ACCEPTANCE

Dr Elisabeth Kübler-Ross was a psychiatrist, author, and pioneer of hospice care. She devoted her entire working life to understanding the nature of death and dying, and identified five states of being that are experienced when grieving:

Denial: This can't be happening.

Anger: I am angry at the world because it is happening.

Bargaining: If I do x, then please don't let y happen.

Depression: The first stage of emotional acceptance.

Acceptance: The point at which the grieving person finally accepts the reality of the situation.

It is helpful to recognize these stages, because everyone experiences them differently and at a different pace. When in the depths of despair, it can be hard to believe that your feelings will ever shift, and that you might ever experience happiness again. But the reality is, if we are patient with ourselves, it is possible both to accept what has happened and continue to feel love for those you have lost; it is possible to experience new happiness without compromising the strength of the feelings that you had before.

ESCAPING LONELINESS

"Every man has his secret sorrows which the world knows not; and oftentimes we call a man cold when he is only sad."

Henry Wadsworth Longfellow

Have you ever had the experience of suddenly realizing that someone you once knew hasn't been in touch for some time? How did you react? Did you feel rejected by their apparent lack of interest? Did you send them a text or pick up the phone? Or did you think, they can call me? All too often we take another's silence as personal rejection instead of stopping to consider what might be going on in their life.

Loneliness and happiness are rarely companions; when one appears, the other tends to leave the building. Humans are by nature social creatures. When we are feeling sad or lonely, other people's joy and laughter can feel like weapons, sent to mock our own sense of isolation from the world. On the other hand, rediscovering a sense of happiness can make loneliness feel like a thing of the past—almost instantly; our troubles seem more manageable; life feels worth living.

How does one state become the other; and how can a helping hand be offered to those who feel cut off from the world?

Many people are happy to spend time alone; it can be enriching to spend quiet time in thought or contemplation, or simply to feel free to enjoy personal space without interruption. Alone time and loneliness are totally different things. Being alone is a choice; whereas loneliness, like grief, feels more like being cut adrift.

The dark thud of loneliness can lead to terrible feelings of emptiness and isolation. It is painful, and for some people leads to problems with alcohol or drugs; it may lead to depression and a lack of self-care; it has triggered some people to violence. As hurdles go, loneliness may seem one of the highest, but in reality, it is less of a hurdle and more of a barrier—and an invisible one at that.

All too often the lonely person will push people away, sometimes with anger, and try not to register their concern, refusing any help, however well-meant. But there are steps away from loneliness that can be taken, if the person who is suffering is willing to give them a try.

> **Rediscovering a sense of happiness can make loneliness feel like a thing of the past, almost instantly.**

HELLO WORLD

Some people become lonely because they are grieving for the loss of a partner; others may feel cut off from old friends; or be too shy to feel confident in company, and believe they don't "fit in" with others. Some who are facing a difficult time in life may cut themselves off, not wanting their troubles to be a burden to others.

At the heart of someone's loneliness may be an inability to share emotions, or trust other people; beneath the outer shell may lie a lack of self-confidence or a sense of feeling unlovable. It can be hard to ask others for help when you are feeling so alone.

You cannot walk toward happiness and loneliness at the same time. They live at opposite ends of the same road. The first step toward happiness involves taking a conscious step forward, without giving a backward glance.

Here are some things to think about, to help overcome loneliness:

* Take some time to focus on your feelings, to understand what is making you feel this way. Learning how to practice meditation can be immensely helpful.

* Try not to reject invitations or offers of help. Those who feel lonely will often push people away. They are afraid to let others get too close.

* Arrange to meet an old friend. You are much more likely to tell someone what is really going on if you spend proper time with them, have eye contact, and know they are listening to you.

* Trust is the key to building relationships. When you are ready, take a risk, and tell someone what is really going on in your life. This could be a medical practitioner or a nurse if you want to be 100 percent certain of confidentiality.

* Taking up walking, running, or any form of mildly aerobic exercise can help to beat the blues. It will help to increase the levels of endorphins in your body, and give you a natural lift.

* Could some aspects of your own behavior be unhelpful to you? Are you adding to your own sense of isolation?

* Are you making an effort to look good? Even when you are at home alone it can make a difference to how you feel about yourself. Do you need help with overeating, drinking, or other issues?

* Pay attention to small things in your life that give you pleasure —birdsong, color, a piece of music—and focus on their detail.

* Don't let yourself stay indoors all day. Go outside, be in the company of other people.

* A good laugh works wonders—do you have a favorite movie that is guaranteed to make you laugh?

* No man is an island. Try not to do everything alone or unsupported.

DANGEROUS JEALOUSY

"Oh beware, my Lord, of jealousy;
it is the green-eyed monster ..."

Iago to Othello (William Shakespeare)

As Othello learned to his cost in Shakespeare's play, jealousy has the power to destroy lives, and takes away the happiness of the one who is consumed by jealous imaginings. Both jealousy and envy are so intrinsic to human nature that they are counseled against in religious teachings. Learning how to deal with them when they strike can make the difference between living a life with full and joyous heart and carrying around a heart that is angry and shrivelling. That sounds melodramatic—but for many people the impact is dramatic.

Envy is the result of wanting what someone else has, or comparing your situation with another person's and finding something wanting in your own circumstances. It can happen at any stage in life and can hit quite suddenly. Jealousy is the emotional response to someone else having what you feel is rightly yours. It is one

> We know we love our friends, but sometimes the differences in your lives makes it hard to relate to one another as you used to.

of the oddities of being human that, as adults, we can feel completely content with our lives until suddenly confronted with someone who has made different life choices and who has what we envisaged for ourselves.

* You bump into former boyfriend and take a dislike to his new partner, even though you have barely spoken to her.

* You have been looking forward to seeing your sister, but pick a fight over a petty detail to divert from your envy that she can afford a wonderful holiday.

* You are excited to be going to a school reunion, but the evening leaves you feeling deflated because your former classmates' lives seem to be more successful than your own.

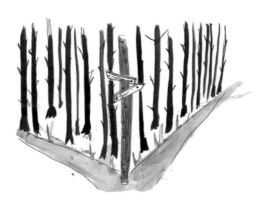

* You feel angry with yourself for feeling jealous instead of happy when your best friend announces she is pregnant—because you want children of your own.

We may think we have left sibling rivalry in our childhood, but it has a habit of raising its head from time to time. We know we love our friends, but sometimes the choices we make in life make it harder to relate to one another as we used to. Jealousy and envy are dangerous companions because they tend to hang out with the dark forces of discontent and misery, leaving less space for happiness to shine a light.

A TIME FOR SELF-REFLECTION

Jealousy and envy are the enemies of happiness because they focus on the things we feel are missing in our lives—often the things over which we have no control. When we compare ourselves with others, we find ourselves wanting (literally). A momentary pang of discontent can be a motivator; it might awaken the competitive part of you that shouts, "I want that; I can do that, too." If it spurs you into action to bring about a change that you definitely want, the impact can be very positive. But if comparisons leave you feeling angry or sorry for yourself, there are a few other solutions to try:

* Pay attention to your body. Notice how you are feeling, and which areas of your body are being most affected. Are you feeling angry,

We choose our own responses to the opportunities we are given.

tense, sad, frightened? Are you feeling the sensation in your stomach, your shoulders, your jaw, your heart?

* Take a deep breath and move your body. Shake your arms; jump on the spot; force yourself to smile; go for a run; find somewhere to shout in private, or to cry.

* Do something physical to shift the tension and encourage yourself to relax. (Reaching for a drink, the chocolate, or ramping up the speed while you go for a drive, are not such constructive reactions.)

* Consider the choices that you would have had to make to achieve what you are coveting. Do you regret having made alternative decisions? Can you find it within yourself to forgive yourself and move on?

* Consider the life or situation you have now. What is it that you are dissatisfied with? What steps can you take to change things? When will you begin?

* What aspects of your life or situation make you happy? What would you not be without? Give yourself space to reflect on these and be thankful that you are blessed.

* Many people find exercise or meditation to be useful—to release physical tension and help focus your mind on what truly has meaning in your life.

> **Happiness begins from within. Others cannot give us happiness, and nor can they take it away.**

Happiness begins from within. Others cannot give us happiness, and nor can they take it away. It is impossible to feel truly happy and fulfilled while we are jealous or wishing ill on others. In undermining their contentment, we diminish our own.

We choose our own responses to the opportunities we are given; we can also choose whether to hold on to negative feelings that are not helping us to live to the full or let them go. To echo the words of St Francis of Assisi, joy arises from accepting the things we cannot change and finding it within ourselves to change the things we can. There will always be people who appear to have more than we do. We can only wish others as much happiness as we would like for ourselves.

CHAPTER 4

THE SECRETS OF HAPPINESS

THE SECRET OF ENTHUSIASM

"Who are we being, that our children's eyes are not shining?"

Benjamin Zander

Benjamin Zander is a world-renowned conductor, teacher, and author of an inspirational book, *The Art of Possibility*. He holds an unshakeable belief that 100 percent of the world's population can be encouraged to love classical music, and his enthusiasm makes it easy  for others to be caught up in his excitement for his subject. He makes people laugh and feel happy as they listen to him, and because he leads, they are happy to follow. His passion enriches lives.

In his memorable talk at a TED conference in 2008 (these are annual conferences devoted to ideas and creativity in the fields of technology, education, and design,) Zander spoke of his realization that, "the role of the conductor is not to make a sound, but to awaken the art of the possible in other people." And that is the power of enthusiasm. When someone cares so much about something, it is easy for others to feel that energy and be invigorated by it.

Benjamin Zander's litmus test to tell that he has brought the crowd with him, is to look in people's eyes. As he says, if their eyes are not shining, he has to question what he needs to do differently.

His words are inspiring because his is a philosophy that could bring happiness to the whole world. What if, instead of focusing so much on our own happiness, we focused on making others' happiness possible? What if, instead of aiming small and wanting one or two people to be happy, we all aimed big and worked to make the whole world happy? Could this work? How can it happen?

In order to have an impact, we need to focus on influencing those around us; they will then go on to influence the people they know, and so the ripple effect continues.

KEEP YOUR EYES SHINING

* **See the world through a young child's eyes.** Young children have a sense of wonder. They are discovering the world for the first time and feel the earth's vibrations more loudly than an adult feels them. Their sense of what is possible is unquestioning.

* **Remain curious.** It is hard to be truly happy when we think we know it all. Knowing it all shuts the door on new experiences. Enthusiasm and excitement, on the other hand, are spurred by anticipation of the unknown.

* **Think of others' happiness before your own.** If everyone's mission on this earth was to help others to become happy first, what an incentive that would be to speed up the process. If none

of us could be happy until everyone else was happy, what would we do first to increase happiness for the greatest number of people?

❋ **Look and listen more closely.** We live life at such a fast pace that we rarely find time to take stock, or stop for long enough to realize the effect we are having on others. But if you start to pay attention to the things you say throughout the day, you will start to notice your impact: Do those around you start to smile? Or do they frown? Are you lifting people's spirits, so they notice their own skills and gifts? Or do they feel deflated and worried by what you say? The words we use and the tone we choose has an effect on the people we meet and spend time with, in every moment of every day. Make it your mission to make people smile, no matter how unlike smiling you may feel. If when you leave, their eyes are shining, the chances are you will have had a positive impact on the next person they meet as well.

What if we all aimed big...

...and worked to make the whole world happy?

The Lottery of Life

When people are asked which would make them happier, winning the lottery or spending life confined to a wheelchair, the vast majority will choose the lottery win—and in the short term they would be correct. In a scientifically controlled study. however, it was found that neither change makes a fundamental difference to people's levels of happiness in the longer term. Six months after winning the lottery or being wheelchair-bound both groups of people were equally happy. Happiness is not something that happens to us, it comes from within.

Are you lifting people's spirits, so they notice their own skills and gifts

THINK LIKE A LOTTERY WINNER

If you were to win the lottery tomorrow, how would you feel? What would you do to celebrate? Would you invest your winnings, share them, spend them? After the initial euphoria passed, what do you think you would value the most about your home, your friends, your family—and the world? Would anything have changed in your life?

The lottery mentality is interesting because it encourages us to think in extremes. By pushing the limits of our imagination we tap into another part of ourselves that tends to be restrained by daily commitments, habits of thought, and financial circumstances. It may not be possible to improve the material side of your life overnight—but you don't need to wait until you win the lottery to start becoming the person you would ideally like to be.

Try asking yourself:

* What are you putting off doing 'until' the conditions are right, that you could start doing right now?

* What could you do for someone else, that would make them feel as if it was their lucky day?

* In what ways are you already a lottery winner?

* What are the keys to unlocking your more adventurous side?

ENJOY THE JOURNEY

"Now and then it's good to pause in our pursuit of happiness and just be happy."
Guillaume Apollinaire

Omar Havana is an international photojournalist with a social conscience. His striking images do more for human rights than speeches and editorial could ever do alone. His series of images of families scratching a living in a vast Cambodian landfill site have been seen by millions around the world. Among these, one picture in particular stands out. A young girl, aged about four, stands alone in the middle of an endless ocean of debris. With a tatty sack in her hands, she looks directly at his camera and smiles, her face lit up in joy. Was it the novelty of being noticed, and having her photo taken? Partly, perhaps. But what touches your heart when looking at his picture is the sense that this little girl, who knows no way of life other than dire poverty, seems rich in her soul—because she knows how to be happy.

> Even in times of crisis, it is possible to find something to laugh at, or something to appreciate—when we pay attention.

For those of us who have the opportunity to choose our journey in life, such an image is a real wake-up call. Who are we to feel less than satisfied with life when others need so much and yet find contentment in what they've got?

Children in general seem pre-programed for happiness. They have the power of imagination to help if something happens to ruin their day. Children talk in superlatives—and they really notice the details. When something is in favor, it is immediately "best" or "favorite" and essential to life (although things may fall out of favor just as quickly.) Can you still remember your favorite childhood toy, picture book, or TV program? That part of your journey is etched in your memory forever.

As adults, we tend to swap play and imagination for the routine of work and a busy diary. The nine to five all too often becomes a means to an end rather than a conscious journey. We no longer pay attention to the detail and don't always fully absorb the joy that our journey is giving us. Our challenge is to spend less time focused solely on the task or the rewards and more on noticing the happiness to be had in the present moment.

When we look back over the course of life, it will not be the detail of the profit and loss sheet, the pressure of deadlines, or the escalating cost of groceries that you will remember—it will be the great times with friends, the joy of watching your children in the school play, a special day in a beautiful location, the joy of walking your dog, the first time you heard your favorite piece of music, shared moments with loved ones. Even in times of crisis, it is possible to find something to laugh at, or something to appreciate—when we pay attention.

KEEP A HAPPINESS JOURNAL

Writers and artists will often keep notebooks or draw sketches of things that have caught their attention. I know a wonderful woman in her eighties who keeps a "thinks book" to capture her memories of the past and record each day's events that give her pause for thought. The inner journey that we travel in life has the potential to be endlessly rich and varied; it provides opportunities to explore and develop our true selves in a way that can open up our minds to new opportunities of who we are and what we might be.

Blogging, tweeting, and other social media have their role to play but sometimes, when we share our thoughts with the world, we offer the edited version. We present ourselves as we would like to be seen, rather than revealing what we really feel.

Deciding to keep a happiness journal can be a wonderful way of tuning in to the here and now and reminding yourself to pay attention to the present. Getting into the habit of writing down,

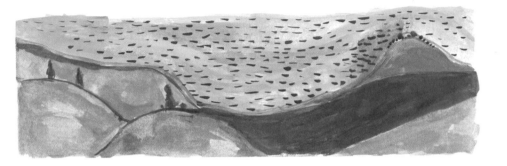

photographing, painting, or capturing in some way those moments when you have felt alive, content, or joyful has several benefits:

* You will immediately feel the experience more intensely, as you seek to capture it.

* Your happiness radar will increase its powers of detection. The more you look, the more you will see reasons to be happy.

* It will serve as a record of happy moments and as a pick-me-up for those times when you feel blue.

* It will encourage you to think beyond the experience of the moment, to make connections between different experiences, and to learn more about yourself.

> The inner journey that we travel in life has the potential to be endlessly rich and varied.

Of course, over time, some of the things that have brought you joy may also turn out to be a source of sadness as you recall times gone by, but the value of capturing the moment when it's fresh is that you can remind yourself of how you felt on that day—and treasure the memory.

THE GIFT OF CURIOSITY

"The mind is not a vessel to be filled, but a fire to be kindled."
Plutarch

Have you ever noticed an animal's reaction when something new is brought into their environment? Their first impulse is to sniff it, pounce on it, chew it, or otherwise explore it, in an attempt to conquer it and make it their own. Even the most elderly cat will muster up the whiskers to check out a new arrival or test the limits of a new object. Just watching the ritual can be amusing but it is interesting, too, to see how alive the animal becomes as it adjusts its perception and learns something new about its world.

Children love the joy of new things. The anticipation of a fun day out can be all-consuming. They are endlessly curious about what other people are doing and saying, and how other children are playing; but they can become bored just as quickly, once familiarity has killed the novelty. The excitement of something new makes children active, bouncy, and happy, and hungry to know more; the disappointment of boredom a little later makes them slump, cry, or become still.

As we grow older, our tendency is to become jaded by novelty. We may forget that life can be fun; we think we have seen it all before. We judge new experiences by the things we have already seen and done, but in doing so we potentially close our minds to enjoying life or seeing things in a new way. Our sense of enthusiasm becomes dulled around the edges. Not only do we stop learning new things, we start to forget the things we already know.

Curiosity stimulates the brain and feeds creativity; new experiences keep us feeling young at heart and lively in spirit. Think of people you know who are creative, and chances are they like to mix things up a little. They might be a bit disordered and impulsive, but life just seems a bit more fun when they are around. The people who have retained their sense of curiosity are the comedians, musicians, artists, writers, and others among us who bring spontaneous joy and laughter into our world.

MIX IT UP, CHEER IT UP

Happiness thrives on variety and fun. Resist the temptation to keep everything the same. Here are a few warning signs that you might be getting a little set in your ways—and some ideas for resetting the dial to youthful curiosity:

✳ **When did you last go out of your way to watch a firework display? If it was cold, did you brave the weather and feel a sense of excitement, or did you watch from indoors, or turn away?**

* What is your reaction to major snowfall? Do you think of it as an obstacle to be cleared or as a winter playground—for you, as well as the kids?

* What is the age range of your friends and acquaintances? Are most of them of the same generation as you?

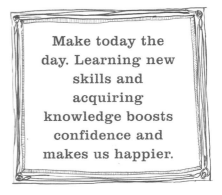

Make today the day. Learning new skills and acquiring knowledge boosts confidence and makes us happier.

* Have you ever dreamed of learning to skydive, dance, ride a horse, or a motorcycle? Have you had a hankering to travel, to run a marathon, or climb a mountain? What excuses have you been putting in your way? Do you want to look back in years to come and regret that you never tried? Or are you willing to take a risk and stretch your boundaries for the sake of curiosity and the risk of happiness?

* When is the last time you learned something new? Make today the day. Learning new skills and acquiring knowledge boosts confidence and makes us happier.

SPIRITUAL AWARENESS

"He whose face gives no light, shall never become a star."
William Blake

Many people lose their sense of happiness because they come to believe their life has no meaning. There are as many reasons for this as there are people on the planet. To paraphrase Tolstoy, every lost person becomes lost in their own way. For many, this sense of loss stems from an absence of spiritual influence in their lives. We are spiritual as well as physical beings, and can communicate by using our senses and mind—but in order to do so, we need to become aware of, and be back in tune with, our soul.

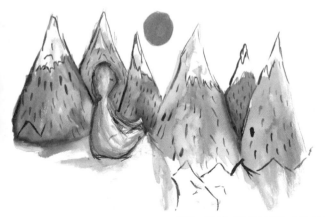

Scientists such as Martin Seligman, who have devoted their professional lives to understanding the nature of happiness, focus more on the mind than on the notion of soul, but they have discovered that those who succeed in living a purposeful life are the happiest.

A purposeful life tends to mean one that is focused on a goal or a mission that is greater than the needs of the individual alone. Altruism and selflessness enhance the chosen path. Great spiritual leaders, such as Mother Theresa, the Dalai Lama, and Archbishop Desmond Tutu, and more secular leaders, such as Nelson Mandela, Gandhi, and Aung San Suu Kyi, all display a calm hinterland and a sense of purpose that give them a spiritual quality. They are acting for the greater good; the quest to improve the wellbeing of others has overtaken any inclination to focus solely on their own needs.

> **Those who succeed in living a purposeful life are the happiest.**

For many, spiritual awareness involves a ritual of worship. Prayers, chants, hymns, and offerings of thanks play an important role in every doctrine. The vibration, rhythm, and symbolism of each stage of the process have a profound effect on the human mind and body. These ancient ways make the body resonate, literally, with the power of the words and music. Those with greater understanding explain that it is by resonating at a higher level that it is possible to become in tune with the Divine.

Those who seek spiritual awareness are seekers after the ultimate truths in life; they are willing to give themselves over to a higher power and to have faith in life's greater purpose. Many on the path to spiritual happiness are searching for a state of bliss. Ironically, differences in spiritual doctrine and rigid adherence to the rules of religious dogma have been at the heart of wars, church schisms, civil unrest, and societies' prejudice for centuries. We seem no closer to universal peace and understanding now than at the time when religion began.

However, for the awakened soul, spirituality transcends dogma. Spirituality has little to do with the differences in the way we worship, and has everything to do with those aspects of our natures that are universal and that, at best, make human beings a force for good, and happiness epitomized.

In the words of St Thomas Aquinas, "To one who has faith, no explanation is necessary; to one without faith, no explanation is possible."

AWAKENING TO SPIRITUAL HAPPINESS

There are many and varied paths leading to spiritual awareness and everyone has to find their own way to meaning. Each religious tradition has its own set of belief systems and rituals, although at the heart of each doctrine the principles and basic practice are fundamentally the same:

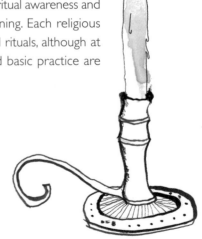

* Belief in a higher power

* Faith

* Time devoted to learning about spiritual matters

* A general belief in our need to love one another as fellow human beings and to strive for a fairer and better world

* A ritual of prayer and devotion that has the power to make people feel closer to their higher power and stronger within themselves

* A call for a simple life, free of possessions and the trappings of materialism

* The teaching that we should love others more than ourselves

Do we need to give up everything and devote our lives to prayer in order to develop spiritual awareness? That question is set to run and run. There is simplicity and freedom in having nothing, which those who have spent time traveling the globe understand well. When we have few or no possessions, we become truly equal. Envy and dissatisfaction disappear. We become more connected to mankind. But something more than that is at work. Spiritual awareness for most people means acknowledging something greater than ourselves—a force of love that encourages us to be humble and put the needs of our own ego to one side for others and the common good.

Every so often we are privileged to meet someone who seems to shine with an inner glow, whose kindness and selflessness come not only from the heart, but from a place inside that seems to connect with the greater good and needs of humanity. These are the people who always care about others; whose words of wisdom have a way of soothing trouble and lifting people's spirits; whose faith in something other than themselves seems to fill them with strength in adversity. They have discovered the power of happiness in the art of spiritual awareness.

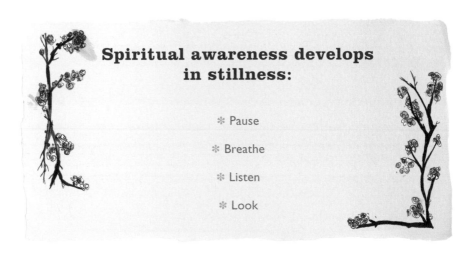

Spiritual awareness develops in stillness:

✳ Pause

✳ Breathe

✳ Listen

✳ Look

APPRECIATE
YOUR UNIQUENESS

*"There is nothing you have to do, get or be in order
to be happy."*
Srikumar Rao

Everything you need to be happy today or in the future lies within you right now. Wishing you were someone else with other talents and skills, or regretting that you did or didn't make a certain decision, will take you further away from happiness. Looking yourself in the eye and appreciating who you are with all your beauty, skills, and potential, will take you to wherever you have the determination to be.

While I was drafting this text, the London 2012 Paralympics were in full flow. Athletes who had overcome a range of physical and mental challenges had come together from all over the world to compete with others who were the best in the world. The

Paralympics showed that disabilities that would challenge many to remain positive are no barrier to success—tenacity, focus, training, guts, and skill gave each person a unique opportunity to succeed.

> **Everything you need to be happy today or in the future lies within you right now.**

At the University of Pennsylvania in the USA, leading psychologist Dr Martin Seligman and colleagues are compiling an ongoing study into the factors that create authentic happiness. Online questionnaires can be completed by anyone who registers online.

Seligman has found that one of the most important conditions of happiness is having strong awareness and appreciation of our own talents. When we understand what we are good at, we become more confident in our competence, and happier in ourselves.

Appreciating your uniqueness requires you to pay as much attention to yourself as you would to other people; it means listening to the complimentary things that people might say and believing that there is merit in them. It also means absorbing criticism, no matter how hard it is to hear, and realizing that there are things about yourself that you might choose to improve or change.

WHO ARE YOU?

* How would you describe yourself in a single sentence?

* Do you describe yourself according to your role at work? As a parent?
  Or as an individual with unique talents?

* What are your strongest personality traits?
  For example, would you call yourself trustworthy?
  Loyal? Strong? Determined? Hardworking? Kind?
  Fair? Tolerant? Brave?

* Give yourself a minute to write down
  all the words you associate with
  yourself, and then divide them into
  positive and negative.

* Consider the negative list and reframe
  each word in a way that shows it to be
  a positive skill in some circumstances.

* Create a Happiness CV, focusing solely
  on your personal path. Write down
  your unique list of achievements, as far
  back as you can remember. Organize it

by date and by year. Include vacations you have arranged, events shared with friends, things you have enjoyed doing on your own, with children, your partner, your pets. Include your work achievements, if you like. Wherever you have been and whatever you have done in your life that has made you happy, proud, or respected—capture it on paper.

✳ Look at the list again. What skills, interests, outlook, or passions are central to your CV? What are the themes that continue to appear? Being sociable? Enjoying art, music, theatre, sport? Studying? Gardening? Making people feel safe and nurtured?

✳ You may find this process stays with you for some time. New things will come to mind and provide another brushstroke for the picture.

You are a unique combination of personal traits, physical and mental skills, attitudes and abilities that make you who you are. By recognizing and celebrating these, you will be better able to channel your attention in a direction that will be fulfilling, and also make you happy.

THE ART OF GIVING

*"The best way to cheer yourself is to try
to cheer someone else up."*

Mark Twain

There is a secret to giving that not everyone has discovered but which is a source of optimism for the world. The good news is that giving to others is good for you. It will make you happy. It will make you feel better about yourself.

I spoke recently to someone whose mother had moved to a smaller home. Sorting through all her possessions and deciding what to let go had been painful for both of them. Even passing books and goods on to a thrift store had proved a hard adjustment. But the charity they chose runs a scheme whereby donors are sent an update on how much money their items have raised. Receiving these letters made my friend's mother so happy that over time she began to give away even more.

In 2010, the Charities Aid Foundation (CAF) joined with *The Sunday Times* to ask 69 of the UK's wealthiest people about the reasons for their philanthropy. The majority said the main reason was that they enjoyed giving. Over half wanted to leave a positive legacy. In the United States, Bill Gates is leading the way via the Bill

and Melinda Gates Foundation. He has personally donated millions of dollars, and, with Warren Buffett, has launched "The Giving Pledge," inviting billionaires to make a moral pledge to leave at least 50 percent of their fortunes as a legacy to philanthropic causes. Media mogul Simon Cowell has been quoted in the past as crediting Oprah Winfrey for helping him to discover how good it makes you feel to give money away as well as make it.

But giving isn't just about money. The most valuable gift of all is your personal time—time spent in the service of others, listening and paying attention. The concept of service may seem old fashioned in the modern world, but the nature of service goes much deeper than the odd good deed. When we are able to serve others, modestly, but putting the needs of the ego to one side, we become more humble, less focused on self, and more aware of the strengths of those around us.

The Good Deeds Pledge

✳ Consider pledging to yourself and others today that you will consciously do one good deed per day, no matter how small, for the next ten days; and that, at the end of those ten days, you will repeat the pledge.

✳ Make a list of deeds done and ask yourself whether or not each one made you happy.

✳ It may turn out to be the best good deed you have ever done for yourself.

The most valuable gift of all is your time.

THE POWER OF CALM

"Many people think excitement is happiness ...
But when you are excited you are not peaceful.
True happiness is based on peace."
Thich Nhat Hanh

Finding a place to be still and calm is wonderfully relaxing. Finding your way to a place of calm inside your mind, is to find a place where transformation can occur and peace can be found. This is the role of prayer and meditation and much of the function of spiritual rituals. The aim is to change your state of mind from a place of busy-ness to one of stillness and contemplation.

Some people find a more active route to calm, via yoga, tai chi, chanting, or running. I find my own path to stillness by walking through the countryside or city in the cool of the morning, although those with more wisdom than I tell me that this is not the same as sitting still and allowing your thoughts to find their own way to resolution.

We all need periods of calm and quiet order. In those moments when we are simply still, transition takes place and things become clearer in our minds.

For some, meditation is the way to stillness. Finding your own route within yourself will take time and practice. It is a skill I have yet to master, but what I do know is how clearly it has transformed the lives of other people, and the tangible benefits they find it provides.

Ella, a writer and speaker, finds meditation helps her to focus, brings new ideas into her mind, and gives her a greater depth of understanding in her work.

Sue, a PR consultant, says her meditation practice provides her with a period of deep calm amid the pace and pressure of each day. It reduces her blood pressure and puts her back in touch with herself.

Rick, a businessman, makes a conscious effort to set aside time for meditation practice each day. On the days when it is not possible, he finds he is less able to control his feelings of annoyance; he is less focused and feels less grounded. Meditation is a vital part of his commitment to inviting peace and happiness into his life.

JUST BREATHE

At its simplest level, finding a route to calm is about breathing. Choose a place where there is no likelihood of interruption or distractions and that is neither too hot nor too cold.

* Lie down on your back on the floor.

* Let your feet flop outward and relax your hands so that your palms, facing up, and fingers find their own natural position.

* Close your eyes and relax your mind.

* Don't worry about where your thoughts are taking you. Don't focus on them. Just let them come and go as they please.

* Focus on your breath.

* Breathe in deeply; and then breathe out fully; breathe in fully and breathe out fully.

* Let your breath find its own rhythm, but keep the breaths deep.

* Maintain this for as long as you feel comfortable.

* Focus only on your breath.

> **Some people find a more active route to calm, via yoga, tai chi, chanting, or running.**

You may find that when you first try to do this, you fall asleep. You may find, too, that your breath is coming from your upper body instead of your lower diaphragm and that you are holding your breath instead of letting it flow. Try to practice breathing with your hand on your belly. It should inflate with the in-breath and deflate with the out-breath. It will come with practice.

THE MAGIC OF LAUGHTER

"When the first baby laughed for the first time, its laugh broke into a thousand pieces, and they all went skipping about, and that was the beginning of fairies."

J.M. Barrie, *Peter Pan*

Happiness and laughter are the Fred Astaire and Ginger Rogers of contentment. Where laughter leads, happiness follows (although not necessarily backward, or in high heels.)

Genuine laughter transforms the body's energy. Someone who is convulsed with laughter literally shakes. Belly laughs are called belly laughs for a reason—they come from deep within the body and are a release of energy.

Of course, not all laughter is a force for good. Some laughter is mocking or dark. Laughter is very close to tears sometimes. Those who work in the medical world will often develop a macabre sense of humor, to protect themselves from the emotional impact of the tragedies they see each day. We laugh when our hearts are breaking because we don't dare to give in to the feelings that will take over if we don't. But in the course of finding happiness, laughter is about letting go of the dark side and finding our way to the light and joy of each day.

Lorna was a talented artist, but by the time I met her, when she was in her late 80s, she was hampered by poor eyesight and arthritis, so was no longer able to paint or walk unassisted. However, she loved the natural world and with her artist's eye for observation and detail she was still inspired and entertained by what she could see—both in her mind's eye and in reality.

Her greatest pleasure was to sit by the window and watch the birds forage for food and go about their daily rituals. She recognized each one and gave them names, and was constantly amused by their antics. I would be told hilarious tales of the latest happenings in the bird world each time I visited her. As she often used to say, it was her sense of the absurd that made life enjoyable. Without her ability to look on the funny side of life, her older age would have been far more painful.

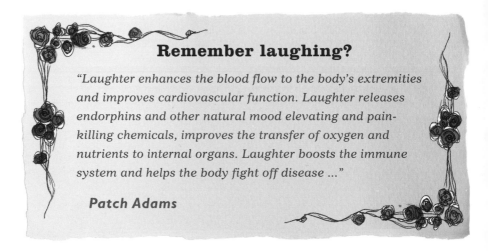

Remember laughing?

"Laughter enhances the blood flow to the body's extremities and improves cardiovascular function. Laughter releases endorphins and other natural mood elevating and pain-killing chemicals, improves the transfer of oxygen and nutrients to internal organs. Laughter boosts the immune system and helps the body fight off disease ..."

Patch Adams

THE FUNNY SIDE OF LIFE

When we are tense, we become very serious—but turning things around in your mind can be a great way to change your mood and find the lighter side of life.

* Check your laughter meter. When is the last time you had a really great laugh? Do you know what makes you laugh? Consider treating yourself to a self-styled comedy night. Hire the funniest film you can find and allow yourself to remember what it feels like to laugh just for the sake of it.

* When is the last time you laughed at yourself? When is the last time someone else had a laugh at your expense, without you taking it personally? Is there a chance you take yourself too seriously? Do you need to lighten up a bit in order to enjoy life?

* The giggle factor. Remember what it was like to be so overcome with giggles that it was impossible to speak? It seemed to happen daily in our teenage years with friends. If you have a favorite giggling partner, ring them up for a good laugh. Recalling old times and chuckling about new ones is a wonderful shortcut to happiness.

> **Happiness and laughter are the Fred Astaire and Ginger Rogers of contentment.**

ACCEPTANCE

"A wise man is content with his lot, whatever it may be,
without wishing for what he has not."
Seneca

It is human nature to have some regrets. Not every choice we make will lead to the outcome we would ideally prefer, but to remain rooted in "I wish" or be forever looking backward to the "might have beens" is to live in a place of lost opportunity. Living a life of regret leads to discontentment and unhappiness.

The next time you hear yourself saying, "I'd love to, but I can't because …," check out your true motives. Are you sure you can't? Or are you making excuses? Is it possible that you are choosing not to do the very thing you think is beyond your control? Part of the process of acceptance is to recognize our fears and the obstacles that we put in our own way—for a multitude of perfectly understandable reasons.

The route to happiness is "to accept the things we cannot change" and to "change the things we can."

Is there a disconnection between the "you" you see in your mind and the "you" you see in reality? Often when answering this question we discover that in some ways, we need to stop being who everyone else thinks we should be, and start being true to our selves.

Do you accept yourself for who you are? We all have flaws. Even if you have made some choices that have led to disappointing outcomes, the chances are that you made them in good faith. You are worthy of your own respect.

If you have done things that you regret, consider what it would take to change that situation. Do you need to ask someone for forgiveness? Do you need to forgive yourself?

Acceptance begins when you realize that you cannot change the past but you can alter your response to it. Change begins with the acceptance that you cannot control everything that happens in your life but you can change your reaction to it and mind your deeds.

MIND YOUR THOUGHTS, MIND YOUR DEEDS

The following step by step process is based on Jungian principles and Joseph Campbell's concept of the hero's journey. It was introduced to me by my friend Florence Hamilton, who is a skilled psychotherapist. She suggests that the journey can be drawn, painted, imagined, or mapped out like a journey of discovery, or a personal expedition. Understanding the concept intellectually is not enough—at least five minutes' practice per day is needed to bring about acceptance of yourself and your situation.

How to take a personal journey of discovery

1. Realize that something has to change.

2. Find a personal guide. This can take the form of professional help, or it can be someone or something you imagine.

3. Surrender to the stream of life. When you're feeling stuck, this is hard to do, especially if you are responsible for others. So find a gentle way to pay attention to your own needs.

4. Deal with your demons. They will come into your mind. Instead of judging yourself harshly, choose to learn from them and find the wisdom in their lesson.

5. Dark night of the soul. It can be cyclical but always has positive implications—even if it's the end of this phase of your life.

6. Connection with meaning. What gives your life meaning?

7. The return to yourself. You will come back changed.

WAKING UP TO EMPATHY

"We have no more right to consume happiness without producing it than to consume wealth without producing it."

George Bernard Shaw

Empathy is the capacity to understand the world from another's point of view. It is not about feeling sorry for someone or judging them; it is the ability to realize, "I have my opinion, but I can appreciate why you might see the situation differently."

Seeing the world through another's eyes lies at the heart of our capacity for kindness, community, kinship, and ultimately, happiness. Unless we can feel compassion for other people's troubles; unless we can try to appreciate what it must feel like to see things from other perspectives, we are simply islands—separated from one another by our indifference and selfishness.

Empathy is quite a sophisticated skill. We are not born with it. The frontal lobes of the brain are the area that helps us to develop reasoning skills, take responsibility, and apply our intelligence. They begin to develop at about two years old, which is also when we start to understand that not everyone sees the world the same way we do. The brain develops the capacity for empathy over time as we learn to share, take turns, forgive, and appreciate each other's differences. Empathy turns our focus outward instead of inward and helps us to be more understanding.

Why does empathy help us to find happiness? When we tune into other people's moods, we pick up on them, and they affect our own sense of well-being. Just as we can be affected by someone else's sadness, so too we can pick up on his or her feelings of happiness. When we are able to make other people feel happy, some of it rubs off on us. That explains why we tend to enjoy the company of upbeat, happy people.

Put Yourself in Others' Shoes

* **Suspend judgment.** Is there someone in your work or social life whose attitude drives you crazy? Does someone close to you irritate you with some of their habits and points of view? Try to suspend your judgment of them for a while and put yourself in their shoes. Why do you think they feel the need to be this way? Is it simply a defense mechanism? What does your irritation say about you? Is there something that you need to change?

* **Lighten up your language.** Who do you know who makes others feel happy to be around them? Listen to their choice of language; hear how they talk to other people. Are they using a lot of humor? Do they tend to frame things in a positive way and give credit where credit is due?

* **Look forward with hindsight**. There are times when being empathetic is challenging. If another driver were to run into your car, it might be hard to choose to see things from their point of view, but getting into a battle of words wouldn't resolve the situation any more quickly. In fact, it may make it worse. Try to look forward to a point where you can forgive their misjudgment; try to use empathy to let go of your anger, so that even if the car was badly damaged, the lasting impact would be on the vehicle, not on you.

Empathy is quite a sophisticated skill.

We are not born with it.

LOVING KINDNESS

"Love is that condition in which the happiness of another person is essential to your own."
Robert A. Heinlein

When we are young children, our own needs are all-consuming. Our focus is on our own comfort and survival; all else is secondary. As we grow older and our minds open and develop, we come to understand that the needs of other people are as important as our own. With this realization comes the richness of appreciating other people and being appreciated ourselves; friendships grow; sacrifices are made for the greater good of a situation, and we discover that taking care of other people's needs reaps its own rewards. We feel loved, connected, of value, and appreciated; and it can make us feel good about ourselves, too. Happiness grows with loving kindness.

The concept of loving kindness lies at the heart of all faiths around the world. It focuses on paying loving attention to the needs of others—and loving them as ourselves. Loving kindness is not about selfless martyrdom but encourages us to use wise discernment in deciding how to act in any situation—with empathy, compassion, forgiveness, love, and understanding. In Buddhism it is known as Metta, in Sanskrit it is Maitreya. The Dalai Lama talks and writes about the steps toward loving kindness that are central to learning to follow a spiritual path.

Each of us has the capacity for loving kindness, but sometimes it is consciously suppressed, due to an event that has happened in our lives. Perhaps a difficult decision taken at work has caused someone pain or hardship; perhaps a choice made in our personal life has had a negative impact on others; perhaps something so painful or hurtful has happened that we can't bear to look at it too closely. When life is tough, we toughen up to get through. Sometimes the walls of self-protection remain in place to prevent us from looking too closely at what has happened.

We discover that taking care of other people's needs reaps its own rewards.

FINDING YOUR PATH

❋ Loving kindness begins with forgiveness, in a way that allows you to make peace with yourself. No life is free of regrets. When we hang on to negative thoughts about ourselves, it becomes harder to act with love toward others, because the heart is closed and in pain.

❋ Learn to sit with your feelings. Sit upright and comfortable, with your legs side by side and the soles of your feet flat and grounded on the floor. Simply be still, and relax your mind and body. Allow whatever thoughts and feelings that enter your mind to be present. Don't try to analyze or judge them; just be aware of how you are feeling and what is happening in your body. Sit with them until they pass. Most of the time we are not even aware of what we are feeling, so learning simply to "be" will help you to become more in tune with yourself. This may take five or 10 minutes.

❋ Wish someone well whom you care about. Think of someone close to you. Consider the traits you appreciate about him or her; think of them with love and care; send them loving and kind thoughts and wish them well.

❋ Wish someone well whom you don't know. Think of someone who is familiar to you, but whom you don't know personally. You have neither positive nor negative feelings about him or her. Send loving and kind thoughts to wish them well, either in your mind or out loud.

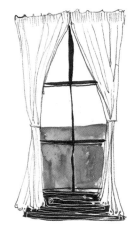

* Wish someone well whom you find difficult. Consider someone whom you find hard to be with, or who has aggrieved you in some way. Consider your feelings of anger or resentment. Acknowledge those feelings and let them change and go. Send this person loving and kind thoughts. Wish him or her well, and wish them happiness.

* Wish loving kindness upon the world. Draw together in your mind these three people and yourself. Wish each of them well and extend loving kindness to the greater Universe. Try to spread your intention equally, without favoring one person more than another. Acknowledge that we are all connected, and that by offering loving kindness to one person, it can be extended to the world.

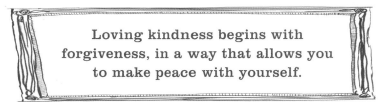

Loving kindness begins with forgiveness, in a way that allows you to make peace with yourself.

If there is to be peace in the world,

There must be peace among nations.

If there is to be peace among nations,

There must be peace in the cities.

If there is to be peace in the cities,

There must be peace between neighbors.

If there is to be peace between neighbors,

There must be peace in the home.

If there is to be peace in the home,

There must be peace in your heart.

Lao Tsu

THE RELATIONSHIP DANCE

"Love does not consist of gazing into each other's eyes, but looking together in the same direction."

Antoine de Saint-Exupéry

The quest for love and happiness is universal. It begins in babyhood, where the close bond formed between baby and mother is instinctive, overwhelming, and based on survival. The kind of loving we have as young children influences the way our brain is wired and helps to form our character; it has an impact on our teenage and adult choices, when the search for a loving relationship begins.

There is a romantic myth that tells us relationships are built on "happy ever after," but the reality is rather more complicated, and potentially more rewarding. Human beings are not fixed in their development; they are forever changing. So whatever form your relationship takes will change constantly.

Love in its early stages is often about looking for points of similarity and connection; personal differences are overlooked or modified or tolerated;

For those who learn to dance in step and with good heart, a loving relationship can be ever more rewarding.

communication is intense and constant; happiness is easily won in exchange for a look or a kiss; the couple are looking for reasons to spend more time together rather than push each other away. Such intensity of feeling is hard to sustain unchallenged. At some point, the rhythm changes and real life comes into play, and then choices and compromises have to be made.

LEARNING THE STEPS

Are you paying attention? Are you paying your partner enough attention, or do you take each other for granted? Are you truly communicating with each other, or are you just passing the time of day? Pressure at work may mean that office demands take over; the challenge of raising children and running a home may take their toll; the passionate intensity of the relationship may shift, leaving a couple wondering whether their connection was built on physical attraction rather than love, after all. Where are your priorities? Ask yourself, what are you willing to do to help things to change?

> **There is a romantic myth that tells us relationships are built on "happy ever after," but the reality is rather more complicated.**

Do you think "we" or "me"? Ask many people what they mean by happiness and they will describe things that provide them with calm, serenity, a sense of euphoria, or a feeling of belonging.

Achieving this state in a relationship takes time. The difference between building a relationship and living parallel lives lies in the willingness to respect each other's needs, and finding the ground where mutual agreement can be found. When you have a disagreement, does love win the day, or does your hurt pride put up a wall of resistance? Do you think in terms of "my needs versus your needs" or is your focus more on "what are our needs?" For those who learn to dance in step and with good heart, a loving relationship can be ever more rewarding.

Are you ready to be happy? Seeking love may begin as a search for perfection. To be happy with who you have found usually requires a bit of adjustment and compromise. Ask yourself what you most love about the person you are with. What are you ready to build together? Can you appreciate each other's strengths and differences? Do you share similar goals? Do you share values? Are the two of you together greater than the two of you apart? Be honest with yourself—and stay in rhythm with the call of your heart.

TAKING A RISK

"You cannot protect yourself from sadness without protecting yourself from happiness."

Jonathan Safran Foer

Have you the courage to let go of the person you think you are right now in order to find happiness? Are you brave enough to live life to the full? For most of our lives, we may choose to live within a personal comfort zone of familiarity and safety; in doing so we think we remain safe from harm and away from failure. But the truth is that the safer we feel, the more afraid we become, because doing something unfamiliar feels increasingly daunting. A very safe life can become an anxious life, lived within self-limiting boundaries. Happiness may become unhappiness because we are not living a life that is fulfilled. Interestingly, it is when we risk failure that we learn the most; and it is when we start to stretch ourselves that our potential for happiness increases.

WHAT HAVE YOU GOT TO LOSE?

* What is your attitude to new situations? Do you embrace them fully
  and worry about the consequences afterwards; or do you choose
  not to try because you don't want to risk failure? Whatever your
  attitude, decide on a new challenge and choose to behave in a way
  that is opposite to your usual behavior. If you are risk averse, just say
  yes to the opportunity; if you usually leap before thinking, decide this
  time to ask advice or create a plan. The new risk-taker may discover
  that she is better at thinking on her feet than she realized; the new
  planner may discover that when fully prepared, she can achieve even
  greater heights.

* What role do you play? Sometimes we are so attached to a particular
  view of ourselves that we don't
  realize that it is holding us
  back. What words do you use
  to describe yourself? Are you
  the shy one, the sporty one, the
  clever one, the one who is
  hopeless at x, y, or z? Where do
  the origins of those beliefs
  come from? Are they really

> Sometimes we are so
> attached to a
> particular view of
> ourselves that we don't
> realize that it is
> holding us back.

true? What opportunities are you not taking because you can't see yourself in the role? How does it feel to try on some other labels for size, such as, I have courage, I have talent, I have the tenacity to succeed, I am a dancer, I am a singer, I am good at sport, I am an

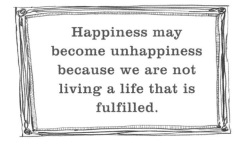

Happiness may become unhappiness because we are not living a life that is fulfilled.

attractive person, I am sociable, I am happy. The brain appreciates clear direction and will fulfill your new instructions if you keep repeating them over a period of time.

Being Our Best

There are several different kinds of happiness, but the hardest won are those moments resulting from an extreme of effort, where we have learned something new, achieved a long-term goal, have done battle with ourselves or our environment—and won. Doing your best and achieving the outcome you hoped for reaps long-term rewards. It is a state of happiness well earned and well deserved.

THE JOY OF FRIENDSHIP

"Happiness quite unshared can scarcely be called happiness; it has no taste."

Charlotte Brontë

According to scientific studies, teenagers show greater levels of self-esteem, personal motivation, strength of character, and levels of happiness when they are with their friends than in any other situation. It doesn't take a research project to figure that out, you may think—but interestingly, the same applies to adults. When adults spend periods of time with friends, they become more intensely happy than when they are with their partner, spouse, or children.

Friends are a vitally important ingredient for happiness. They bear witness to our lives and tell us stories of our own past. They help us to form and fulfill our dreams. They laugh with us, comfort us, and party with us—and they give us a boost when we're feeling low. Friends are part of our story and our journey. They remind us of who we are when we have lost our way.

But friendships, like gardens, need to be tended and cared for in order to grow. They can be all too easily squandered through inadvertent neglect, especially as we get older and allow the routine of life or the needs of our families to get in the way.

NURTURING YOUR FRIENDSHIPS

The round table of friendship. Whose friendship do you value in your life and why? Who would you turn to in a crisis—or to have a great time? Think of your circle of friends as King Arthur's knights of the round table: who would be sitting around the table with you, and why? When you bring each friend to mind, ask yourself why you value that person, and whether you have done enough to show how much he or she means to you. Do your friends know that you value them so highly? Perhaps it's time you let them know.

What makes you a good friend? When you think of yourself in relation to your friends, do you like what you see? Are you the kind of person who always provides a listening ear? Are you a leader who makes things happen? Are you the nurturer who always soothes the way? What could you do more of that would make people happier? What could you do less of that would make someone's day?

> **Do your friends know that you value them so highly? Perhaps it's time you let them know.**

Staying in touch. Don't leave staying in touch to chance. Always make sure that you have friends' addresses. In the Facebook age it is easier to stay in touch with people than ever before, but commenting on each other's news or posting some news of your own is not enough for a friendship to flourish. Speaking, writing, or seeing each other will have far more impact.

Friendships, like gardens, need to be tended and cared for in order to grow.

CARING FOR OTHERS

"Happiness is a perfume you cannot pour on others without getting some on yourself."

Ralph Waldo Emerson

Many parents will say their greatest source of joy and happiness is providing for and loving their children. Mothers undergo a physical as well as an emotional transformation to give birth which contributes to the special bond of loving care that they feel. For many, the role of father, mother, home-maker, provider, or carer—in whatever form that takes—is not only a personal role, it becomes their main reason for being, and a purpose for life.

Caring for others is a vital part of many people's professions. Nurses, care workers, teachers, and social workers have all chosen professions where the needs of others are the central focal point of every day. Happiness comes, not necessarily from the task, which can be demanding and sometimes exhausting, but from the sense of purpose, the sense of belonging, and the gratitude that is bestowed in return.

> **Caring for others delivers gratitude in the short term and happiness in the long term.**

Caring for others delivers gratitude

Pledge with a happy heart to do as you say.

in the short term and happiness in the long term. It may take a child their entire lifetime to realize how tenderly they were cared for; an elderly person may be too encumbered by pain to recognize who is looking after them, until the pain subsides; a teacher may never get the thanks he deserves, but may gain satisfaction from students' positive exam results, or noticing that someone they once taught has risen to professional success.

The Selfish Gift of Altruism

* How easy do you find it to put the needs of others before your own? How happy does it make you feel?

* When is the last time you cared for someone, without expecting thanks in return. Did the feeling of wellbeing outweigh your wish for gratitude?

* Think of three things, however large or small, that you could do for someone today. Write them down, and pledge with a happy heart to do as you say.

CHAPTER 5

HOW TO LIVE A HAPPY LIFE

OPERATION HAPPINESS

"We all live with the objective of being happy; our lives are all different and yet the same."

Anne Frank

Happiness is as invisible as electricity, and just as powerful. We can feel its effects and see its impact, but everyone's description of what it does will be different. When happy people smile or speak their radiance can light up a room. Their warmth makes everyone more tolerant of others' views and foibles. When we are happy, we glow and we are beautiful, and more things feel possible.

But happiness can be turned off very suddenly, as surely as blowing out a candle. The moment we choose to invest importance in things that are outside our control, we put our happiness at risk. We begin to focus on what we want, and when we do not get it, we feel disappointment, or a sense of loss and failure. If the goal or desire is important to us and is closely aligned to our sense of who we are as individuals, it can be hard not to feel diminished when things don't quite turn out as planned. In low moments it can feel as if happiness will never return.

What can we do to turn things around? How is it that some people are able to live their lives with contentment, no matter what life throws at them, while others are left buffeted and devastated by disappointments and feel constantly let down by life.

Every life includes periods of sadness and disappointment. Darkness and grief have a way of throwing shadows when we shine light upon their surface, which conjure up self-doubt and imaginings. Unhappiness can send ripples across the years and trigger other memories; the current loss may remind us of all losses; the current "failure" may turn the whole of life into a failure. Each disappointment may have a physical and personal impact long after the cause of the original sadness has been consigned to history.

> **When we are happy, we glow and we are beautiful, and more things feel possible.**

The danger when we are in the grip of grief or sadness or despair is that in our determination to be independent we build walls around ourselves that are so high others cannot reach us. Not only are we without happiness, we are alone. For a minority, the pain that this causes can be catastrophic. They will turn to ways to numb that pain rather than sit with it a moment longer.

But it doesn't have to be that way. Developing the habit of positive thoughts and actions can shore us up for more challenging times. As we grow in resilience, so we grow in understanding. As Eleanor Roosevelt once said, "A woman is like a tea-bag. She won't know how strong she is until you put her in hot water." And the same is true of men.

Find Engagement and Meaning

"Optimism is invaluable for the meaningful life. With a firm belief in a positive future you can throw yourself into the service of that which is larger than you are."

Martin Seligman

Professor Martin Seligman has devoted his professional life to reframing the way that psychology is used and viewed. He has been at the forefront of the concept of "positive thinking" and his work has developed the field of psychology so that it focuses as much upon making well people happier as it does on influencing those with depression or other conditions.

His research has found that there are three main types of happy life:

✻ The pleasant life. Finding as many ways as possible to create a life of pleasure; seeking positive influences and developing positive emotions to enhance our experiences in life.

✻ The good life. Living a life of engagement—via our work, or by finding purpose in raising a family; knowing what your strengths are and using them to live life in a state of flow.

✳ The meaningful life. Using your unique skills and talents for the greater good.

A life of engagement and meaning is enhanced by pleasure; but a life of pleasure alone is not the most successful route to finding happiness. This is because we become used to the feeling of pleasure. The initial feeling of euphoria diminishes when the pleasure is repeated without the presence of engagement or meaning—just as the first chocolate out of the box tastes delicious and leaves us wanting more but eating the whole box at one sitting diminishes the memory of the first taste and leaves us feeling uncomfortable into the bargain.

Martin Seligman has found that the difference between optimists and pessimists lies in their view of how long the effect of something negative is going to last. A pessimist believes that the impact will last a lifetime, whereas an optimist believes that the effect is time-bound in the short term and need not impact on outcomes in the future.

SHAPE UP FOR HAPPINESS

"A bear however hard he tries, grows tubby without exercise."
Winnie-the-Pooh

Exercise is good for you in more ways than one. It tones your body, keeps you healthy, and it boosts your mood, which in turn helps self-esteem and self-confidence. And let's face it, when we feel good about ourselves, we feel happier too, which leads to a positive frame of mind.

In Traditional Chinese Medicine (TCM) the body's life force and energy levels are known as chi. Our chi levels have a dramatic impact on our well-being and on the organs of the body. When we are feeling happy, our levels of chi increase; the body functions more healthily, and a positive cycle ensues. In western medicine, we measure the levels of endorphins, serotonin, dopamine, and adrenaline produced by the body. These, too, increase when we are happy.

> **Exercise is a great way to lift your mood and balance your emotions.**

However, when we are feeling low, the opposite happens. We have a tendency to eat the wrong foods, slow down, and hold tension in the body. Our blood flow slows, which means the body does not process and expel toxins. The levels of happy chemicals reduce; our levels of chi energy reduce; the body becomes out of balance and we are more likely to feel low, weepy, or depressed.

As little as 30 minutes of exercise has been shown to lift a depressed mood or enhance happiness and self-confidence. Exercise is a great way to lift your mood and balance your emotions.

MOOD BOOSTERS

Are you getting enough exercise? Even walking the dog or a brisk stroll around the block a few times a day is a good start. The heart is a pump, which needs to be exercised to work at its best. When the blood is circulating properly around the body, it supports all the essential organs of the body, and clears out the waste and toxins. It increases the level of oxygen to the body and brain.

Many complementary therapies focus on increasing chi levels and getting the body back into balance. Techniques such as aromatherapy, reflexology, reiki, and acupuncture can all be beneficial for releasing energy blocks and easing the mind. If you want to reduce the level of stress and tension in your body while learning to improve concentration and focus, yoga stretches and breathwork can be very beneficial. Balancing calm healing processes with regular cardiovascular exercise will shape up the heart and lungs, reoxygenate the blood by making it flow faster and more freely, and trigger the release of "feel good" chemicals, such as dopamine, endorphins, and serotonin.

Change Your Lenses

"Ninety percent of long-term happiness levels are predicted not by what happens to us, but by the way your brain processes the world."

Shawn Achor

Shawn Achor is author of The Happiness Advantage *and CEO of Good Think Inc. His work turns the conventional success formula on its head. Rather than hard work delivering happiness and satisfaction, he believes that happiness increases our capacity for hard work. His study of the connection between our levels of happiness and its direct effect on our productivity has had an impact not only on individuals but on companies and on the world of finance. He has spoken to business leaders in over 45 countries, offering them*

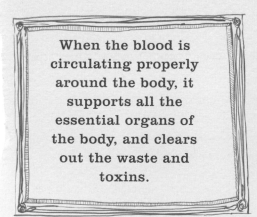

When the blood is circulating properly around the body, it supports all the essential organs of the body, and clears out the waste and toxins.

evidence for how happiness benefits productivity and the state of the economy.

During the course of his work, Achor has discovered that the majority of people spend a great deal of time focusing on competition, hassles, disadvantages, and problems rather than paying attention to the positive advantages and opportunities that they might have. We need to change the lenses through which we view the world in order to reframe our impressions with a more positive perspective.

In a simple experiment, he has observed that if people develop the habit of writing down three new things that they are grateful for every single day, that simple act will have a positive influence on the way their brains work in just three months. Thinking positively sends out ripples of influence that offer the world the opportunity to be happier—exponentially.

When we are happy, we are more productive; when we are positive in the present moment, our brains are able to work more effectively. When we are happy, our levels of dopamine increase naturally, which infuses the brain with a more positive way of viewing the world.

SENSING HAPPINESS

"A thing of beauty is a joy for ever."
John Keats

Every day throughout the year, thousands of commuters change trains at Clapham Junction station in south London. It just so happens that several of the platforms face west. So in the autumn months, as the evenings begin to shorten, many are treated to a beautiful sunset while they are waiting for a train. The majority of people keep their heads steadfastly downward, focused on sending texts, reading their book or newspaper; but if they were to choose to look up for a moment, they might see something so beautiful that it would soothe away the troubles of the day in an instant.

Much of what makes us happy is experienced via our senses. Our sight and senses of hearing, taste, touch, and kinaesthetic (physical) awareness send messages to the brain in ways that help us to store and recall memories in milliseconds. A certain perfume might conjure up a favorite friend; the scent of a tree or flower might transport you back to a vacation; the sound of a song

> Once you understand the memories and triggers that boost your experience of happiness, you can begin to make changes to the way you live.

on the radio will take you back to the first time you heard that band; the taste of a fruit might remind you of a meal shared with friends; standing in an airport lounge may remind you of standing in a similar spot to meet someone off a plane.

We are very used to using speech to express our thoughts and feelings, but stimulating our other senses can summon up all kinds of memories, or can be used simply as an immediate mood changer. Equally, sensory deprivation of any sort will have an impact on how we experience life, and our sense of well-being.

Take a moment to answer the following questions:

✳ What does happiness feel like to you?

✳ What does it look like?

✳ What color is it?

✳ What does it sound like?

✳ What does it taste like?

When you think about your current environment, which senses are being stimulated in a way that gives you enjoyment, and which are being starved? If you love music, when is the last time you turned on your stereo and played your music loudly enough to appreciate it properly? If happiness feels like being close to someone, when is the last time you gave someone you care about a huge hug? If you love the taste of food, how often do you cook up a meal for friends? If happiness is the color green, can you make time to go for a long country walk? If happiness looks like becoming a home owner, what steps do you need to take to make it happen? Once you understand the memories and triggers that boost your experience of happiness, you can begin to make changes to the way you live.

RE-TUNE YOUR SENSES

The healing power of color. Do you have a favorite color? Are you aware of different colors affecting your mood?

Color results when lightwaves are absorbed or reflected at different frequencies. Our brain translates the frequencies into the color we see via color transmitters in the eye. Many complementary healers use color as a tool for healing. Bright colors are used to sell products; for example, yellow in particular is used to help house sales.

So why, when we have so many beautiful colors to choose from, do most people insist on wearing black? Black is the color of convenience and funerals—and style. Bright colors, on the other

> **Raise the vibration of your day by wearing something bright and colorful.**

hand, are for carnivals and gardens, summer days and party nights. Colors send a message about our mood and frame of mind.

If you are feeling a bit fed up, resist the temptation to camouflage your mood by wearing black. Instead, choose to raise the vibration of your day by wearing something bright and colorful. The chances are, not only will you feel more cheerful, those around you will notice and appreciate the splash of brightness, too.

The magic of music. Music moves people. It can uplift and energize as easily as it can trigger sadness or romance. I was once sent a CD as a thank you from a young client. It was a compilation of favorite happy songs from old musicals, and featured tracks such as "The bare necessities" and "Singing in the rain." He called it "A Gift of Happiness" and it was. It had me smiling from beginning to end.

What would be your top 10 happiness tracks? Try writing them down. Consider creating your own CD compilation to deliver instant happiness at times when you need a helping hand.

CELEBRATE YOUR LIFE

"Happiness is not a goal … it's a by-product of a life well lived."

Eleanor Roosevelt

A close friend recently celebrated a milestone birthday. She decided to invite all her female friends from every stage of her life for one big girly knees-up. Her husband and her children played host and it was a joyous and sometimes riotous evening that grew into a whole weekend. Looking around the room, it was like seeing a picture of different stages of her life in microcosm.

A few months later she was diagnosed with a brain tumour, and she faced that terrifying time with her characteristic positivity and bravery. Fortunately, she has recovered fully and is in fine health once more. But looking back on the ups and downs of her life—and her year—she commented, "I was so happy at my party. I looked around the room at all the friends who were there, and I thought to myself, "It has all been all right. I have done a good job. My life has been

> **Aging has very little to do with the passing of the years, and everything to do with the nature of the spirit within.**

worthwhile. I love my family; my husband and I are still enjoying life together; my children are well balanced and happy, and soon to be embarking on their own lives; and I am surrounded by friends whom I love and who have witnessed my life with all its ups and downs. I have been so lucky, and I am so happy with my life."

What I loved and respected about her words was her ability to notice and appreciate the importance of that moment. She saw that all the actions and decisions she had taken over the course of her life had led to that moment of recognition and celebration. She hadn't arranged the party as a review of her life; she arranged it to have fun and enjoy the company of friends, and to celebrate a mid-life coming of age. But in taking the time to reflect on that shared moment with other people, she realized how happy she was and that her life so far had been lived to the full.

EMBRACE AGING

There is great beauty to be seen in a "lived-in" face. Every line and wrinkle tells a story. Many older people have a gentle radiance that cannot be applied cosmetically; it develops through the wisdom of years, through understanding the nature of love, and the gaining of experience. Aging has very little to do with the passing of the years, and everything to do with the nature of the spirit within. Aging is no barrier to happiness. Getting older can be a time of liberation, laughter, and fun.

Celebrate good times. As children, we find celebrating easy. A birthday is time for treats, candles, games, and gifts. Celebrations have another purpose, too: they are a ritual that honors a milestone—they are a rite of passage that marks a new phase of life. Rather than ignore your moments in time, honor them and reflect on your journey so far.

Bring your dreams to life. Many people begin to live their lives more safely as they get older. Understandably, they feel more physically vulnerable or less energetic. But there are examples all around the world of healthy

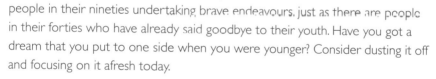

people in their nineties undertaking brave endeavours, just as there are people in their forties who have already said goodbye to their youth. Have you got a dream that you put to one side when you were younger? Consider dusting it off and focusing on it afresh today.

Look forward to your future. When you look back, what will you respect about the choices you have made? And what will you regret that you haven't done? Honor your life by seizing your opportunities. When you make your decisions, don't let age be the excuse that got in your way.

CHAPTER 6

WHAT MAKES YOU HAPPY?

WHAT DOES HAPPINESS MEAN TO YOU?

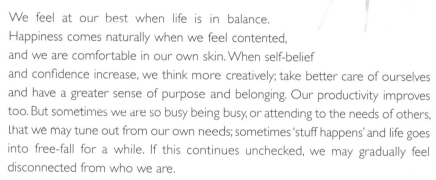

"Happiness is a warm puppy."
Charles M. Schulz

We feel at our best when life is in balance.
Happiness comes naturally when we feel contented,
and we are comfortable in our own skin. When self-belief
and confidence increase, we think more creatively; take better care of ourselves
and have a greater sense of purpose and belonging. Our productivity improves
too. But sometimes we are so busy being busy, or attending to the needs of others,
that we may tune out from our own needs; sometimes 'stuff happens' and life goes
into free-fall for a while. If this continues unchecked, we may gradually feel
disconnected from who we are.

Every single one of us experiences the world differently. We each see the world
through our own unique eyes. That uniqueness is what makes people interesting
and life a pleasure—but it means that what makes each of us happy will differ too.
Happiness is many things to many people, it can mean being yourself; having fun;
enjoying a sense of belonging; loving others; being a friend; appreciating a job well
done; knowing you have done your best; feeling loved and appreciated; enjoying

hobbies; discovering new skills; enjoying new discoveries; accepting the world and your situation as it is; finding contentment in the place where you find yourself now.

Happiness cannot be given to us by someone or something else, it starts from within. Joyfulness grows when we choose to let it in to our lives—and to enable that to happen, you first need to spend a little time considering what happiness means to you.

FINDING JOY

Happiness has a powerful energy that is meant for sharing. It is a force field that can attract others and make them feel happy too. In those moments when we are feeling less than happy, it may feel as if we need to make a dramatic change in order to make a difference. But sometimes the smallest decisions and changes can make the greatest difference. It is a truism that every change begins with a single step.

 * Review your well-being. Reflect on those areas of
    your life that you may have been neglecting.
    What have you been putting off that would
    lighten your heart and increase your well-being?

* Set yourself new challenges. Like a plant that has been pruned or newly planted, we sometimes grow most vigorously when we have been knocked back or choose to begin life anew.

* Make happy plans. We schedule our work, and we note birthdays and other key events on the calendar, but few people choose to set themselves goals for life. Deciding what you want to achieve, where you want to go, and what you want your legacy to be can be very empowering.

> We need to choose to be happy, and to do that, you need to spend a little time considering what happiness means to you.

* Respect your need for a routine. Everything in the natural world has a rhythm. It varies subtly with the seasons, but there is a pattern to each day.

* Look after your health. Your body and mind are connected. You will feel less strain if you look after your physical self, and take care that you have enough sleep, food, and exercise.

* Treat yourself with respect. Sometimes, when we are unhappy, we may take revenge on ourselves by treating ourselves badly, by diminishing

who we are, or becoming angry and pushing others away.

* Believe in yourself. Self-belief increases our ability to achieve the outcome we seek.

* Take action. If you have a goal, choose to commit to it. Focus on changing the things you can.

* Seek acceptance—for those things that you can't change and that are beyond your control.

* Acknowledge your feelings. Happiness is not something you can buy off a shelf; it doesn't turn up on demand; it comes from the heart and may appear when you least expect it.

* Appreciate the contrasts in your life. White looks whiter when it is seen next to black than it does when it is next to grey; times of joy are more intense when you have experienced times of sadness.

* Be patient. There are times when life presents a challenge that is so painful and unexpected that it may feel as if you will never experience happiness again. But patience and understanding are the pathways to hope. It is possible to rediscover joy in time.

* Let go. Of your need for control, for perfection, of your expectation that life should be lived completely on your terms.

* Tune in to the present moment. Look consciously for the good, the positive and the opportunity in the here and now.

* Use the language of happiness. When you use words such as joy, contentment, glee, delight, bliss, gladness, fun, delight, you send signals to other people that lighten their hearts.

* Seek guidance. If you are struggling, reach out to someone who can help you through the tough times; for some that may be a friend, for others a coach or counselor, for others a higher power.

* Be kind—to yourself and others. Kindness and happiness are partners through life. Where one leads, the other always follows.

* Be true to yourself. Happiness lies ultimately in our ability to accept ourselves as we really are.

Being Kind

"Imagine"

John Lennon

One secret of happiness is more effective and more vital to well-being than any other, and that is to be kind to others—not just when you feel like it, or because today is world kindness or happiness day, or because you want to feel good about yourself, but because being kind to others is the only true way for us to find happiness in this world.

In the spirit of John Lennon's song of universal love and hope, imagine what it would be like if everyone was kind, all the time. We are not talking about the home-baked and sugary kind that overindulges and makes us feel slightly queasy. We are talking about habitual kindness; hard to give kindness; being kind before you have received kindness; being kind because it is simply the right thing to do; being kind even if you have a sense of dislike for someone; loving kindness and forgiving kindness.

Kindness lies at the heart of happiness because when we help other people, we feel good about ourselves. Kindness is also an energy for good; those who receive kindness are more likely to give kindness.

PAY ATTENTION TO THE PRESENT MOMENT

"Rather than just liking the smell of roses, or hating the smell of manure, perhaps you could start by appreciating that you have a nose?"

Buddhist wisdom

Your future happiness begins in the present moment. Yesterday has gone; nothing you do or say can change the past—but tomorrow and the days ahead are unchartered territory. There is so much you can do to influence the way your future evolves and what you feel about it.

Living life consciously puts more emphasis on the present moment. It brings our present actions into clear focus; encourages us to mind what we think and to think about what we do and say.

Paying attention to the present moment encourages careful observation and appreciation of the things around us; it puts us in closer touch with our feelings, our reactions, and our intuition, because there are no distractions.

By appreciating the present, we can also choose to be happy with this moment—and recognize with every second, every minute, and every hour that passes that we are right here, right now, and can influence the future—in any way we choose.

Focus Your Attention for Greater Happiness

"The best society is where people are happiest; and the best policy is one that produces the greatest happiness."

Professor Richard Layard

Your future joy and happiness lie in your own heart, mind, and soul. The seeds are planted in the thoughts, dreams, and actions of every day. Only you can know what your happiness looks and feels like. Sometimes it helps to spend time focusing on the kind of future we would prefer. Try asking yourself:

* ✳ I am happiest when...

* ✳ My happiest memories are of...

* ✳ The people who make me happy (and who I need to show my appreciation to) are...

* ✳ My future vision of happiness looks like this...

* ✳ My actions for happiness are...

* ✳ I deserve to be happy because...

ACKNOWLEDGMENTS

Behind the words on the page are those who make me happy and helped to make the book happen: with huge love and thanks to my lovely family and friends for always 'being there'; to my mother (the original Lois) for her proofreading skills (unsurpassed at 80+); in grateful acknowledgment of conversations with inspiring and talented people whose views and knowledge helped me to shape the content; in particular: Tony Buzan, Professor Tanya Byron, Bev James of The Entrepreneurs' Business Academy, and Sir Ken Robinson. My great thanks and appreciation too, to the team at CICO Books for approaching me with the concept, and for their immense creativity and patience—especially Cindy Richards, Clare Sayer, Helen Ridge, and Anna Galkina. Special thanks to Marion Paull for her kindness and great editorial skill, Amy Louise Evans for her charming illustrations, and Teo Connor Studio for such 'happy' graphic design.

There is a plethora of books, videos, and other resources available on the science and roots of happiness, but here are a handful that I found inspiring:

BOOKS

Achor, Shawn *The Happiness Advantage* (Virgin, 2011)

Bienkowski, Andrew *One Life To Give* (Experiment, 2010)

Buzan, Tony *Embracing Change* (BBC Books, 2005)

Csikszentmihaly, Mihaly *Flow: The Psychology of Happiness* (Rider, 2002)

Dalai Lama, The and Howard C. Cutler *The Art of Happiness* (Rider, 1998)

De Saint-Exupéry, Antoine *The Little Prince* (Egmont, 1991)

Ferrucci, Piero *The Power of Kindness* (Tarcher, 2007)

Frank, Anne *The Diary of Anne Frank* (Pan, 1969)

Frankl, Viktor *Man's Search for Meaning* (Rider, 2004)

Gerhardt, Sue *Why Love Matters* (Routledge, 2004)

Gibran, Kahlil *The Prophet* (Arrow, 2005)

Gilbert, Dan *Stumbling on Happiness* (Vintage, 2007)

Hamilton, David R. *Why Kindness Is Good For You* (Hay House, 2010)

James, Bev *Do It! or Ditch It* (Virgin, 2011)

Kaufman, Barry N. *Happiness is a Choice* (Ballentine, 1991)

Long, George (trans) *The Meditations of Marcus Aurelius* (Duncan Baird, 2006)

Milne, A.A. *Winnie-the-Pooh* (Methuen, 1926)

Mountain Dreamer, Oriah *The Invitation* (Thorsons, 1999)

O'Donohue, John *Anam Cara* (Bantam, 1999)

Pilkington, Doris *The Rabbit-Proof Fence* (Miramax 2002)

Rao, Srikumar *Happiness at Work* (McGraw-Hill, 2010)

Robinson, Sir Ken *The Element* (Allen Lane, 2009)

Rubin, Gretchen, *The Happiness Project* (HarperCollins, 2009)

Seligman, Dr Martin *Flourish* (Nicholas Brealey, 2011)

Siegel, Daniel *Mindsight* (Oneworld, 2011)

Zander, Benjamin and Rosamund Stone *The Art of Possibility* (Penguin, 2006)

RESOURCES

The search for Authentic Happiness is ongoing at Penn State University. Those who want to take part in the survey can register for free via the Authentic Happiness website and complete a series of questionnaires:

www.authentichappiness.sas.upenn.edu

The Pursuit-of-Happiness project includes an online quiz and a series of in-depth questionnaires to monitor and measure factors affecting happiness. Visit the happiness quiz at www.pursuit-of-happiness.org

The TED: Ideas worth spreading website contains many illuminating videos on a huge number of diverse subjects. Visit the website at www.TED.com. This is a very short list of the talks I most enjoyed:

Achor, Shawn "The Happy Secret to Better Work," Feb 2012
Csikszentmihaly, Mihaly "Flow: The Secret to Happiness," Oct 2008
Gilbert, Dan "The Surprising Science of Happiness," Sept 2006
Rao, Srikumar "Plug Into Your Hard-wired Happiness," Mar 2010,
Robinson, Sir Ken "Ken Robinson Says Schools Kill Creativity," June 2006
Robinson, Sir Ken "Bring On the Learning Revolution," May 2010
Seligman, Dr Martin "The New Era of Positive Psychology," Jul 2008
Zander, Benjamin "The Transformative Power of Classical Music," Jun 2008

REFERENCES

Many of the opening quotes were sourced from www.goodreads.com. Original sources are included here where it has been possible to research them:

Page 7: The Declaration of Independence can be accessed via The National Archives, www.archives.gov

Page 24: quote from *The Peach Keeper* by Sarah Addison Allen (Hodder, 2012)

Page 25: The fear-busting exercise is adapted from an approach used by Bev James in *Do It! or Ditch It* (Virgin, 2011)

Page 30: More recent data can be found at www.happiness360.org

Page 31 on Bhutan was influenced by an article by in the *Independent Magazine* by Andrew Buncome, 14 January 2012

Page 32: The Happy Planet Index is at www.happyplanetindex.org

Page 36 refers to Rimer J, Dwan K, Lawlor DA, Greig CA, McMurdo M, Morley W, Mead GE. 'Exercise for depression'. Cochrane Database of Systematic Reviews 2012, Issue 7. Art. No.: CD004366. DOI: 10.1002/14651858.CD004366.pub5

Page 41: Bärbel Mohr (1964-2010) was the author of *The Cosmic Ordering Service* (Mobius, 2006) and other titles

Page 61: quote ©Gretchen Rubin, founder of The Happiness Project, www.happiness-project.com

Page 84: Omar Havana's photographs can be viewed at: www.omarhavana.com

Page 98: Mackenzie, Susan 'Sharing the Wealth: *The Sunday Times* Giving Index,' June 2007, issue 29